Guided by Spirit

A Guidebook for Enhancing Mediumship and Psychic Skills

Rev. Colleen Irwin

All Rights Reserved. Copyright © 2025 by Rev. Colleen Irwin
www.TalkWithColleen.com

All rights reserved. No part of this publication may be reproduced or distributed in any form or by any means, or stored in a database or retrieval system, without the prior permission of the publisher.

colleen@irwinsjournal.com

ISBN: **979-8-9994753-0-5**

Printed in the United States of America

Table of Contents

Introduction	5
What is a Development Circle?	8
Types of Development Circles	9
Development Circle Best Practices	10
How a Circle Could Look/Feel	14
Facilitator's Resource Kit	16
Finding the Right Circle	20
Circle of One	22
For Experienced Circle Leader	24
Instructions for Starting a Circle without a Leader	25
How to Use the Lessons	30
Lesson 1 – Grounding Protection & Prayers	31
Lesson 2 – Energy, Meditation & Mindfulness	41
Lesson 3 – Healing & Mediumship	49
Lesson 4 – Intuition	57
Lesson 5 – Signs & Symbols	65
Lesson 6 – Working with the Senses – The Clairs	73
Six Lesson Review	81
Lesson 7 – Spirituality & Mediumship	83
Lesson 8 – Tools in Your Tool Chest (For Mediums)	93
Lesson 9 – Building Confidence	103
Lesson 10 – Ethics & Responsibilities	111
Lesson 11 – Telepathy, Precognition & Remote Viewing	121
Lesson 12 – Self-care for Mediums	129
Full Circle: Self-Test	137
Full Circle: Weaving It All Together	142
Meditations for Use	144
Group Based Activities	150
Self-Exploration Exercises	156
Journal Prompts	158
Topics to Discuss	159
Books and Other Resources	160
30 Day – Spirit Awareness Journal	162
30 Day – Gratitude Journal	168

$$\begin{bmatrix} \text{For Rev. Jack Rudy} \\ \text{who journeyed to Spirit in 2023.} \\ \text{His kindness and loving guidance,} \\ \text{like a beacon, revealed the true} \\ \text{essence of teaching.} \end{bmatrix}$$

Introduction

Welcome to your journey of deepening your connection with Spirit. This Guidebook is here to support you—whether you're developing on your own, guiding a Development Circle, or growing within a spiritual community. Each lesson blends insight with practical exercises to build your skills, increase self-awareness, and strengthen your spiritual connection.

Before I began facilitating, I sat in many Development Circles, learning alongside my mentor, Jack Rudy. Jack's relaxed, Spirit-led style was very different from my structured, organized approach. When I launched a Development Circle in Rochester, NY, in 2018, there was no clear roadmap. I leaned on experience, intuition, and a lot of trial and error. Over time, I came to appreciate Jack's wisdom: Spirit will guide you—whether you're participating or leading.

I also learned something else: many people crave structure. They need practices they can take home—something tangible to hold onto, refer back to, and track their progress. Development doesn't stop when the Zoom call ends or the chairs get stacked.

What you'll find here is a flexible but solid foundation of topics you can return to again and again. It's designed for open circles where participants may change week to week, for groups who rotate leadership, and for individuals studying solo. You'll find support, exercises, and prompts that help keep the momentum going between circles.

There is no gatekeeping here. This Guidebook honors every step of your journey—whether you're just starting out or have years of experience. Some seasoned circle leaders might hold tightly to certain ways of doing things, but here, we embrace openness and flexibility. Everyone's path is unique, and all are welcome to learn, grow, and lead with heart.

You don't need to be the most advanced intuitive in the room. You just need clarity, structure, and heart.

This Guidebook is especially helpful if you're stepping into a leadership role—or preparing to. Anyone who attends circle regularly will tell you: eventually, you'll find yourself guiding one. That's why this isn't just a workbook—it's also a reference.

The Facilitator's Resource Kit provides tools for holding space with direction, safety, and flow—without being controlling. You'll learn how to encourage consistency, deepen spiritual practice, and foster a shared sense of purpose. The real magic happens when development becomes a lifestyle—not just a meeting.

The Work Beneath the Work

Many people come to development circles excited to build their gifts. They want to become mediums, psychics, or healers—and that's beautiful. But what's often misunderstood is this: your spiritual development is not separate from your skill development.

You can't become a strong, clear channel for Spirit by only showing up for two hours a week and expecting to progress. Circle is important—but it's just the beginning. The real growth happens between sessions. It's the hours spent meditating, sitting with your guides, reflecting on your patterns, and healing your emotional wounds that create the foundation for your gifts to unfold.

I've seen it again and again: people get frustrated when their development feels slow, but they haven't done the deeper work. They're waiting for something to click, when in reality they're being invited to go inward.

This path isn't all sunshine and roses. Yes, there is joy, love, and beauty—but first, you must be willing to face what you've been avoiding. To look honestly at what's blocking your connection and commit to healing it.

Everyone's journey is different. Your relationship with Spirit will not look exactly like mine—or anyone else's. That's why it's so important to listen, reflect, and share. A good facilitator can guide you. Circle can support you. But you still have to do the work.

Spiritual development takes patience. And here's the truth I had to learn myself: the more you resist going deeper, the longer it takes to connect. The moment I stopped resisting—when I finally faced what I feared the most—everything changed.

You won't miss your moment. Spirit's timing is perfect. But you must meet it with readiness. The work beneath the work is what shapes you into the spiritual practitioner you are becoming.

These journal prompts serve as gentle companions on your journey, inviting you to look within. Like quiet whispers of the soul, they encourage reflection, ease resistance, and awaken the deep wisdom already present inside you.

Foundations of Spiritual Development

- Why am I truly drawn to develop as a medium, psychic, or healer?
- Do I see spiritual development as optional or essential—and why?
- What beliefs do I hold about what this journey "should" look like?
- How has my definition of "growth" changed over time?
- What do I hope spiritual development will heal or strengthen in me?
- When have I confused skill-building with inner growth?
- What does a spiritually grounded medium look or feel like to me?

Personal Practice

- What is my current routine for spiritual practice?
- Do I connect with Spirit regularly outside of Circle? If not, why?
- How does my relationship with my guides feel right now?
- What practices bring me the most peace or insight?
- Where do I notice avoidance or resistance in my practice?
- How do I stay accountable to my personal development?
- What does "showing up for Spirit" mean in my daily life?

Facing Resistance

- Where in my development journey do I feel stuck or frustrated?
- What fears come up when I think about going deeper?
- Am I waiting for results or actively participating in my own growth?
- What excuses do I tell myself to avoid the harder work?
- When have I rushed a process that needed more time?
- How does impatience show up in my spiritual journey?
- What might change if I allowed myself to go at the pace Spirit offers?

Healing and Integration

- What wounds or patterns have I carried into my spiritual work?
- How do these wounds influence how I receive Spirit?
- What am I still avoiding emotionally or spiritually?
- When have I tried to guide others without being fully ready myself?
- What would it look like to minister from a healed place?
- How can I offer myself more grace as I do the hard inner work?
- What parts of me still need to be seen, acknowledged, or forgiven?

Letting Spirit Lead

- What does spiritual alignment feel like in my body?
- When have I experienced Spirit's perfect timing?
- Where am I still trying to control how things unfold?
- What am I afraid will happen if I surrender more deeply?
- How do I discern the voice of Spirit from my own expectations?
- What would it look like to trust the process more fully?
- How might Spirit be inviting me to grow right now?

What is a Development Circle?

Development Circles are gatherings where individuals come together to enhance their connection with the spirit world. These circles offer a supportive, structured environment for participants to explore their intuitive gifts, practice spirit communication, and deepen their spiritual development, either under the guidance of an experienced medium or as a self-directed group.

The tradition of Development Circles dates back to the mid-19th century, during the rise of the Spiritualist movement. Rooted in the belief that the spirits of the deceased can communicate with the living, Spiritualism gained momentum in 1848 with the Fox Sisters of Hydesville, New York. Their claims of communicating with spirits through rapping sounds captivated the public and sparked widespread interest. Formal Development Circles soon emerged, providing a way for mediums to refine their abilities.

In a typical Development Circle, participants meet regularly — often weekly — to meditate, raise their vibration, and open themselves to spiritual communication. Activities may include exercises to strengthen the "clairs" (clairvoyance, clairaudience, clairsentience, etc.), practice in giving and receiving messages, and discussions on spiritual topics. The collective energy of the group, shaped by intention and shared focus, is believed to enhance each individual's connection to spirit.

Circles are usually held in quiet, controlled environments, allowing participants to safely explore their abilities without distractions. This format encourages collaboration, with members supporting one another's growth through shared experiences and constructive feedback. Though Development Circles have evolved over time, their core purpose remains unchanged: to provide a nurturing space for exploring and developing mediumship. Whether led by a seasoned medium or formed by like-minded individuals, these circles continue to foster personal growth and a profound connection to the spirit world.

Spirit Flows Through You — A Path for All Seekers

Spiritual development is deeply personal — yet it thrives in community. Whether you identify as a Psychic, Medium, Healer, or simply someone exploring your connection with Spirit, you'll find value in the lessons offered here. While there is an emphasis on Mediumship, the insights apply to all aspects of intuitive growth. Every Medium is Psychic, and the truth that Spirit flows through you, not from you is powerful for all on a spiritual path.

This Guidebook honors the unique journey each person takes. No matter where you are on your path, the tools and teachings here are designed to support your growth with clarity, heart, and openness. The work you do in your circle or on your own will deepen your connection and expand your ability to serve Spirit in whatever form that takes.

Types of Development Circles

Mediumship Development Circles vary in focus, structure, and goals. This book emphasizes Mental Mediumship for beginners, but all mediums benefit from revisiting the basics. Below are common types of Development Circles:

Traditional Spiritual Circles
    Focus: General mediumship, including spirit communication, developing the "clairs," and deepening spiritual connections.
    Structure: Open to all levels, regular meetings led by a medium or peer-led.

Beginner Mediumship Circles
    Focus: Foundational knowledge for newcomers, exploring abilities in a supportive, instructional environment.
    Structure: Teaching-focused with guided exercises on the basics of mediumship.

Advanced Mediumship Circles
    Focus: Refining skills and exploring complex techniques for experienced mediums.
    Structure: Led by seasoned mediums with higher expectations for participants.

Evidential Mediumship Circles
    Focus: Providing clear, verifiable evidence from Spirit to validate spirit presence.
    Structure: Emphasizes accuracy and specificity, with regular practice sessions.

Platform Mediumship Circles
    Focus: Public mediumship, including platform etiquette, audience work, and evidence-based messages.
    Structure: Weekly practices designed for those serving Sunday services or public events.

Physical Mediumship Circles
    Focus: Physical phenomena like table tipping, materialization, or direct voice.
    Structure: Highly controlled environments, often in low light or darkness, with energy focused at the center.

Healing Circles
    Focus: Channeling healing energy through spirit guides, combining mediumship and spiritual healing practices.
    Structure: Includes distance or hands-on healing, meditation, and intention setting.

Psychic Development Circles
    Focus: Enhancing psychic abilities like intuition, clairvoyance, and precognition, without focusing on spirit communication.
    Structure: Flexible formats with tailored exercises to develop specific psychic skills.

These circles cater to different aspects of mediumship and psychic growth, allowing you to focus on areas that resonate with your goals. Whether you're a beginner or an advanced practitioner, there's a circle to support your journey.

Development Circle Best Practices

Creating a successful Development Circle involves several key factors that work together to create a supportive and effective environment for growth. While there's no one-size-fits-all approach, certain best practices can help ensure that your circle is both structured and adaptable, meeting the unique needs of its participants. Here are some essential considerations for setting up and maintaining a successful Development Circle:

Define the Purpose and Structure of Your Circle
- **Type of Circle:** The first step is to decide what kind of Development Circle you want to lead. Will it be an open circle, where anyone is welcome to join, or a closed circle, limited to a specific group by invitation only? Open circles can be dynamic and diverse, bringing together a range of experiences, while closed circles often foster deeper bonds and focused development over time.
- **Participant Levels:** Consider whether your circle will cater to a particular experience level—Beginner, Advanced, or Mixed groups. Beginner circles may focus more on foundational skills and confidence-building, while advanced circles can delve into more complex aspects of mediumship. Mixed groups can offer a rich exchange of knowledge, with experienced mediums mentoring those who are newer to the practice.
- **Focus of Mediumship:** Determine whether your circle will concentrate on Physical Mediumship, Mental Mediumship, or a combination of both. This Guidebook is specifically designed to support Mental Mediumship, which involves receiving and interpreting messages from the spirit world through the mind, rather than physical manifestations.

Establish a Consistent Schedule
- **Timing:** Consistency is key to maintaining momentum and commitment within your circle. Decide on a schedule that works best for your group.
    - **Weekly:** A weekly circle helps build regular practice and keeps participants engaged and progressing steadily.
    - **Monthly:** For those with busy schedules, a monthly circle can provide a balance between practice and other commitments, allowing for more in-depth exploration during each session.
    - **Special Sessions:** Consider hosting special all-day sessions or week-long courses for intensive learning and development. These can be particularly effective for diving deep into specific topics or skills.

Foster a Supportive Environment
- A successful Development Circle thrives on a supportive atmosphere where participants feel safe, respected, and encouraged. Establish ground rules for confidentiality and mutual respect, ensuring that everyone has the space to explore their abilities without judgment.
- Encourage open communication, where participants can share their experiences, ask questions, and offer feedback. This not only enhances learning but also strengthens the sense of community within the circle.

Maintain Flexibility
- While structure is important, it's equally crucial to remain flexible. Be prepared to adapt the circle's activities based on the group's needs, energy levels, or specific interests that arise. Flexibility allows for spontaneity and responsiveness, which can lead to unexpected insights and growth.
- One of the best examples of this is the development of the "Act It Out" group exercise I created on page 150. What resulted was several breakthroughs for multiple people in the room, including myself. All because I heard this voice in my head say "abandon what you are doing and create a play for the person who is not understanding what you are saying."

Prepare with the Right Tools
- Equip your circle with a well-stocked resource kit (see page 16 for ideas). Include index cards, oracle or playing cards, dark envelopes, and personal objects for psychometry. Having diverse tools on hand supports varied exercises that meet different learning styles and development needs.
- Customize your resource kit to match your circle's focus—Mental Mediumship, Physical Mediumship, or both. These tools make sessions interactive and help participants connect with their abilities more tangibly.

Commit to the Work Beyond the Circle

Whether you are the facilitator or a participant, it's important to remember that the work doesn't begin and end within the circle's time. True growth and connection require preparation and reflection outside of the weekly gathering.

Facilitators need to spend time preparing lessons, meditations, or exercises to hold a safe and supportive space. Participants benefit most when they dedicate time to personal practices—like meditation, journaling, or connecting with their guides—between sessions.

This outside work strengthens the group and deepens everyone's experience. It's where insight unfolds, challenges are faced, and spiritual growth takes root. Viewing circle as a continuous journey, with small daily steps between sessions, supports steady progress and deeper insight.

What to Charge

Deciding what to charge for your Development Circle is a personal decision that can vary widely depending on your goals, the location, and the needs of your participants. It can be uncomfortable to talk about money, but it is an important consideration when starting a circle.

Leading a Development Circle requires considerable preparation time and energy. The fee you set reflects not just the time spent during the sessions, but also the effort put into planning, organizing, and providing necessary materials. It's important to recognize this as an energy exchange, where contributions support the circle leader's work and help maintain the flow of positive energy within the group.

Accessibility and Ethical Practice
- Some circles operate on a donation model, where participants contribute what they can. Others set fees ranging from $5 to $40 per session, depending on factors like the leader's experience, location, and resources provided.
- For example, beginner circles might charge $5 to $15 per session, while more advanced circles may charge between $20 and $40, reflecting the depth of material and preparation involved.
- To maintain accessibility, you can offer open circles on a donation basis, ensuring everyone can attend, and reserve set fees for more specialized, in-depth circles. This tiered approach balances inclusivity with the value of more intensive work.
- I often do a $10 per person and split the proceeds with the host. This approach keeps the circle affordable while helping sustain the spiritual community.
- It's important to set expectations for contributions in a way that doesn't create pressure or discomfort for participants. Introduce the fee structure or donation system at the start of the circle, explaining the reasoning behind it and emphasizing that contributions are a way to support the collective energy and growth of the group. Make it clear that all contributions, whether monetary or in the form of time and effort, are valued and appreciated.
- Being transparent about fee usage helps build trust. Explain that fees support the venue, preparation time, and material costs. Circle leaders often spend 1-2 hours preparing for each hour of leading, including planning, organizing, and answering questions outside of sessions. This clarity fosters understanding and comfort among participants.

Options for Those Unable to Pay
- To remove financial barriers, consider offering alternatives for those unable to pay. Participants could help with setup, cleanup, or administrative tasks as a form of energy exchange, promoting inclusivity.
- One circle sponsors one person regularly, allowing them to participate without cost. You could also create a scholarship fund for reduced or waived fees.

Pay it Forward

My mentor, Jack Rudy was a master of taking care of those that did not have the financial resources. I was one of the many that he paid a class or covered participation in a circle for. For that reason, I carry that tradition on.

Typical 2 Hour Structure

Two hours seems to be the perfect amount of time to run your circles. It is just at that point in time, that the participants begin to get overwhelmed. Here is how I structure a weekly circle:

- Welcome/Opening Prayer/Introductions: 5-10 minutes
- Topic of the Day: 10 – 40 minutes (dependent on the topic)
- Meditation: 5-15 minutes
- Exercise(s) - Remaining time
- Q & A/Closing Prayer 5-10 minutes

The Why Behind Each Section

These suggestions aren't meant to be exhaustive or mandatory – they're shared to help spark ideas for creating your own circle.

Opening Prayer: While not everyone is used to opening or closing with prayer, beginning each session this way helps set the tone and create sacred space. Rotate different prayers to help participants discover what resonates, and encourage them to create their own.

Introductions: Helps ensure everyone is included in the group, you may wish to have participants send healing to one person and say one thing they are grateful for.

Healing Book: Pass around a healing book for participants to add names of those who need positive energy. This practice fosters a sense of community and compassion.

Gratitude Sharing: Ask participants to introduce themselves and share three things they are grateful for. This practice helps ground the group in positive energy and fosters a supportive atmosphere.

Homework and Journal Review: Invite questions or reflections on the previous week's assignments. This discussion can provide clarity and deepen understanding.

Topic of the Day: Present the day's topic, allowing for flexibility in how deeply you explore it based on the group's interest and energy. Be prepared to adjust the meditation or exercises accordingly. There are times you may forgo both because the discussion is so productive.

Group Based Exercise: Having the group work on an exercise with the entire group or one-one-one helps participants be engaged and reinforces learning. Make sure you leave time at the end to recap and go over the circle.

When you break up in smaller groups, be aware that people can get chatty. Keeping everyone on pace can be a challenge. Don't be afraid to move people around if you see this happening. I have a coach's whistle to gain everyone's attention.

Q&A/Closing Prayer: Before closing, invite questions to support clarity and connection. End with a prayer to gently close the sacred space. Like the opening, this helps participants build the habit of working intentionally with Spirit.

How a Development Circle Could Look/Feel

A Development Circle should provide a welcoming yet structured space for participants to grow their mediumship abilities. Meeting regularly—once a week for up to two hours—is ideal, offering consistency and fostering continuous progress.

The ideal number of participants often sparks debate, but flexibility is key. In my own circles, attendance has ranged from as few as four to as many as 25 participants, and I've heard of even larger groups. Fluctuations in attendance are normal in an open circle and often work to your advantage, as Spirit may guide the circle to focus on the needs of specific participants. I've seen this happen more often than not.

Whether your circle is large or small, a mix of experience levels can be highly beneficial. Experienced mediums can mentor newer participants, while everyone gains from revisiting foundational skills. To accommodate varying attendance and experience levels, consider breaking into smaller groups during larger gatherings. This allows for more personalized attention and gives seasoned participants an opportunity to lead mini circles, building their confidence and offering fresh perspectives. Regular meetings ensure that those who miss a session can easily reconnect and stay engaged.

A well-rounded circle should focus on a variety of skills while regularly revisiting foundational practices. Discussions on ethics and sharing experiences from private readings, events, and platform work can provide valuable insights for all participants. For newer members, these shared experiences offer a deeper understanding of the challenges and nuances of spirit communication. By creating a flexible, supportive environment, your Development Circle can meet the needs of participants at every stage of their mediumship journey while fostering growth, connection, and confidence.

Encourage Growth Through Self-Study

Homework and journaling exercises can help participants deepen their understanding of how Spirit works with them. These assignments, however, are always optional.

Each person develops at their own pace, and it's important to honor this. We all have free will, and the choice to engage with these exercises—or not—will influence the rate of progress. Some may find that consistent practice accelerates their development, while others may take a slower, more reflective approach. Both are valid paths, as mediumship is a deeply personal journey. Participants are encouraged to revisit exercises when they feel ready, often uncovering deeper insights over time. The focus remains on creating a supportive environment where everyone feels encouraged, not pressured, to grow at their own pace.

A Development Circle should always be a nurturing space where participants feel safe exploring their mediumship abilities. Flexibility—in structure and in meeting the needs of attendees—is key. Whether someone attends regularly or sporadically, the circle should remain a welcoming place where they can return, connect with Spirit, and continue their journey of growth.

Development Circle Ground Rules:

Establishing clear ground rules is essential for maintaining a positive vibration and a respectful, focused environment within your Development Circle. These guidelines help ensure that everyone, including Spirit, benefits from the time set aside for learning and growth. Below are the ground rules I've established for my circle, which you are welcome to modify to suit your group's needs. It is not uncommon for circle leaders to lock people out as the circle begins.

Thank you for choosing to be part of our circle. To maintain a harmonious and productive environment, please keep the following in mind:

- **Technology Use:** To maintain focus and minimize distractions, please silence your phones and avoid using any electronic devices during the circle. This ensures that our collective energy remains strong and undisturbed. Take off any electronic devices you may be wearing.
- **Energy and Grounding:** At the beginning of each session, take a moment during the opening prayer to ground yourself. Grounding helps connect us with the earth and stabilizes our energy, creating a solid foundation for the work ahead.
- **Inclusivity:** Our circle is a welcoming space for people of all backgrounds and experience levels. We value diverse perspectives and encourage everyone to share openly and without fear of judgement.
- **Be on Time:** Please arrive on time so we can begin promptly. I understand that unforeseen circumstances may occasionally cause delays, but punctuality is key to respecting others.
- **Late Arrivals:** The seats closest to the door will be reserved for latecomers to minimize disruption. If you arrive after the opening prayer, please take a moment to read the prayer quietly to yourself before joining the circle work.
- **During Meditation:** If the meditation has already begun when you arrive, please wait outside the circle until it is complete. Joining mid-meditation can disrupt the energy and focus of the group. Do not leave the circle during the meditation.
- **Refreshments:** Please bring only water to drink in the circle. This helps maintain a clean and uncluttered space conducive to spiritual work.
- **Respect and Focus:** Give full attention and positive energy to those demonstrating. Remain still and avoid talking, as distractions or speaking out of turn can hinder others' focus and growth.
- **Honest Feedback:** Providing honest and constructive feedback on each other's messages is crucial to our learning process. We grow by understanding what resonates and what might need adjustment. If you do not know — say so.
- **Asking Questions:** No question is unimportant — please feel free to ask anything. While there may be times when I'll move a question to the end of the session, I promise to do my best to address all inquiries.
- **Patience and Sharing:** Remember, we are all at different stages in our development. While it may sometimes feel repetitive to review the basics, it's important to share our experiences and struggles. Often, it's these shared experiences that lead to breakthroughs for others in the group. If I can learn something new every time I lead, so can you.
- **Let go of Judgment.** Together, we create a supportive and inclusive environment where all can grow.
- **Flexibility in Rules:** While these rules help maintain order and respect, there are times when flexibility is necessary. If someone is running late or if an unexpected situation arises, we'll adapt as needed to ensure everyone has the opportunity to participate fully.

What is a Facilitator's Resource Kit ?

As a circle leader, having a well-equipped tool chest can greatly enhance the experiences of your participants. The tools listed here are designed to facilitate a wide range of exercises, helping your group to explore and develop their mediumship abilities. This section provides an overview of the recommended tools and offers suggestions on how to incorporate them into your circle activities.

There are times you may come to circle as the leader with a specific exercise in mind, only to find that you have 3 or 4 new people that the exercise may not work for. Dropping back to an intuition or telepathy exercise may be warranted. Likewise, you may have a group of more advanced participants and your simple exercise is not to their benefit so you switch to something more message centric. More often than not, you will decide as the discussion happens of a perfect exercise — yet you don't have a deck of cards or items for people to read psychometry.

Tools in Your Facilitator's Resource Kit :

Index Cards (Subdivided for Various Exercises):
- Blank: For spontaneous writing, message delivery, or drawing symbols.
- With Quotes: Use for inspiration or as prompts during meditation or message exercises.
- Numbers 0-9 & Letters A-Z: For numerology and letter-based exercises, or random selection during games.
- Famous Dead and Living People: For exercises focused on identifying and connecting with specific spirits or energy.
- Colors, Shapes, Flowers, Modes of Transportation: Use these for symbolism exercises, where participants interpret or receive messages related to these elements.
- Artists, Smells, Tastes, Vegetables, Fruits: For sensory exercises, where participants may explore how different senses or creative energies come into play during mediumship.
- Message Types, Words: Use for exercises in delivering different types of messages or exploring specific words that come through during readings.

Decks of Playing Cards (Three Decks with Different Backs):
- Use for psychometry exercises, where participants hold a card and describe its energy or what they sense about it.
- Use for telepathy exercises, where one participant transmits and the other receives

Dark Colored Envelopes:
- White envelopes participants may see through, so think of the transparency
- Use for blind readings, where participants give a reading on an unknown item or message

Divination Tools, Oracle Cards, Wisdom Cards, Tarot Cards:
- Use these decks to practice divination, intuitive interpretation, or as prompts for deeper message work.
- Pendulums, Divining Rods, Runes, and the like. You never know when they will come in handy.

Postcards, Business Cards etc. :
- Use for exercises where participants describe the energy or history of a location depicted on the postcard.
- Use the cards of people you know well for psychometry exercises, where participants read the energy of the person associated with the card.

Blow-Up Beach Ball:
- Use for group energy exercises, where participants pass the ball around to build and transfer energy within the circle.

Notepaper and Pens:
- Essential for note-taking, message writing, or drawing symbols and impressions during exercises. I keep a variety of pens incase something comes to me to work with.
- Having pens and scratch paper for participants will help them
- Sometimes I bring crayons and paper for participants to touch with their creative side of the brain to help them give messages.

Miscellaneous Items (A Small Container of 30+ Personal Items):
- **Examples Include:** Button, measuring tape, pin, pill box, lipstick, shell, Lego, gum wrapper, matchbox car, cookie cutter, pen, Polly Pocket, old photograph, key, Barbie accessory, bottle cap, old ribbons, etc. The important things here is that they are all deeply connected to you. You know the objects well, and their story. It is a great exercise for students to build confidence.
- **Usage:** These items can be used for psychometry exercises, where participants hold the item and describe its energy, history, or the person associated with it. The personal nature of these items makes them excellent for honing detailed and accurate readings.

Additional Helpful Items: (Easily found on Amazon or Dollar Store)
- Sand timers (30 second, 1 minute, 2 minute, 5 minute) Great for breakout readings so participants can work at their own pace
- Painter's Tape – To mark the floor
- A coaches whistle – To gain participants attention when they breakout
- (4) Small puzzles with large pieces (25 or less pieces)
- Blindfolds
- Toy animals to give people to research animal guides
- Candle to set the intention – I usually light it prior to students arrival. Any candle will work, some people prefer a white candle, I use a Chakra colored one because I like it
- Clock to keep you on pace and aware of the time
- Clipboard, sign-in sheet, blank paper

Using the Resource Kit in Your Development Circle

If you are leading a regular circle, having a "resource kit" of exercises and resources is invaluable. Spirit may guide you to adjust plans based on the needs of the group, and being flexible allows you to make those shifts seamlessly.

Some of the best exercises I've facilitated were spontaneous and created in the moment. Never underestimate the value of these off-the-cuff activities—they often resonate deeply with participants. At times, the exercise you planned may not suit the energy or needs of the group. In those moments, your resource kit provides a backup or inspiration for trying something completely different.

By staying open and adaptable, you can ensure each session supports the growth and connection of your circle, even when plans change.

Integrating Tools into Weekly Sessions:
>Plan your sessions around the tools available in your chest. For example, you might use the index cards one week for a symbolism exercise and the business cards the next week for psychometry.

Flexibility and Creativity:
>Don't be afraid to get creative with the tools. Encourage participants to think outside the box and explore different ways to use the items.

Encouraging Participation:
>Use these tools to foster engagement and hands-on learning. The tactile experience can be a powerful way for participants to connect with their intuitive abilities.

Reflect and Discuss:
>After each exercise, take time for group discussion. Reflect on the experiences, what worked well, and how the tools helped or added to the practice.

Organizing the Facilitator's Resource Kit

Over time, I've tried many ways to organize my kit—starting with a small handled box, then two overloaded banker boxes. Now, I use three photo/craft keepers (14.9x12x5 inches), each with 16 small (4x6 inch) boxes sorted by topic. This lets me bring only what I need, or everything if I want Spirit to guide me in the moment.

Whatever system you choose, make sure it supports ease and flow. Whether it's simple or structured, the goal is to keep your tools accessible, organized, and ready to serve the circle's needs.

Notes

Finding the Right Development Circle

Joining the right Development Circle can greatly impact your growth as a medium. Here are some tips to help you find a circle that aligns with your needs and goals:

Assess Your Needs: Reflect on your experience level and what you hope to gain. Are you a beginner seeking foundational knowledge or an advanced practitioner refining specific skills? Understanding your goals will guide you to the right fit.

Research and Seek Recommendations: Explore local spiritual centers, online communities, and word-of-mouth recommendations from trusted friends, mentors, or fellow practitioners. Personal insights can provide valuable information about a circle's dynamics and effectiveness.

Attend Before Committing: If possible, attend a few sessions before committing. Observe the group's energy, the leader's style, and whether the circle aligns with your goals. Pay attention to how comfortable you feel in the environment.

Consider Leader Styles: Not every leader's style will resonate with you. The right leader can unlock your potential, but finding them may take persistence. I personally attended several circles before discovering one that helped me break free from limitations. Stay patient—the right circle can lead to profound growth.

Seek a Supportive Environment: The best circles foster respect, inclusivity, and open communication. Look for an atmosphere that encourages constructive feedback and values all participants' experiences and perspectives.

Evaluate the Leader's Experience: A knowledgeable and approachable leader can make a significant difference. Look for someone who balances structure with flexibility to support individual growth within the group.

Be Open to Trial and Error: Finding the right circle may take time. Don't be discouraged if your first choice isn't a perfect fit. Explore different options until you find a circle where you feel supported and inspired.

Trust Your Intuition: Your intuition is a powerful guide. If something feels off, move on and try another group. Trust yourself to find the right environment for your development.

Your Journey, Even Without a Circle

This Guidebook is designed with you in mind—even if you don't have a circle right now. As you work through each section, take time to reflect and complete the exercises on your own. When you see questions meant for group discussion, answer them for yourself as part of your personal growth.

If you don't have a circle to join, this book still offers a strong foundation. It can guide you step-by-step to start your own circle when you're ready. Think of it as both your personal development tool and your roadmap to building community.

Online Development Circles: A Modern Approach

In today's digital age, online Development Circles offer a flexible and accessible way to connect with like-minded individuals, no matter where you live. With the right approach, online circles can be just as effective as in-person gatherings.

- Explore online platforms hosted by reputable spiritual organizations or experienced mediums on platforms like Zoom, Microsoft Teams, Skype, or specialized forums. Choose communities that align with your goals and values.

- Ensure you have a reliable internet connection and are comfortable with the required technology. Test your setup beforehand to avoid disruptions.

- Be mindful of time zone differences when selecting a circle. Choose one that fits your schedule to maintain consistency in attendance.

- Treat the online circle with the same respect and commitment as an in-person circle. Create a quiet, distraction-free space where you can focus and participate fully.

- Take advantage of chat features and discussion times to connect with other participants. Online circles can foster strong, supportive communities, just like in-person ones.

- Some circles provide recordings for members who can't attend live. Use these as a resource to revisit lessons and deepen your understanding.

- Respect the virtual space by following the circle's ground rules. Mute your microphone when not speaking, minimize distractions, and remain present throughout the session.

Whether in-person or online, the right Development Circle provides the support, guidance, and community you need to grow in your mediumship journey. Explore your options, trust your intuition, and find the circle that resonates with your path.

Not All Circles Are Equal

Spending time with like-minded people and practicing consistently can build confidence and open new doors. But if a circle isn't helping you grow, it's okay to move on. In my own journey, I tried four or five circles before I found the one that truly supported my development.

I gave each circle three sessions before deciding. When I finally found the right one, something clicked—growth unfolded in ways I never expected.

You can have a transformative experience too, but it may take patience and persistence. If the right circle doesn't appear, you might be called to create it yourself. Give any new group a few sessions to settle in. Sometimes, the magic just needs a little time.

Circle of One

This Guidebook encourages both group engagement and solo practice, welcoming everyone from beginners to experienced practitioners. Even seasoned mediums gain fresh insights and strengthen their abilities by revisiting the basics. Designed as a spiral of growth, this Guidebook invites you to revisit foundational concepts, uncovering new layers of awareness and deepening your connection with Spirit each time.

For solo practitioners and beginners, journaling, meditation, and the solo exercises in each lesson provide a strong foundation. Journaling allows you to record experiences, track insights, and reflect weekly on your progress. Meditation centers the mind and builds awareness of Spirit's presence. Treat each exercise as a chance to learn independently, with Spirit as your guide and partner along the way.

Creating a Supportive Space

A nurturing space for solo practice can significantly enhance your experience. Choose a quiet, comfortable area where you won't be disturbed. Light a candle, hold a crystal, or ground yourself with deep breaths. This supportive environment will help you relax, focus, and strengthen your connection with Spirit.

Weekly Affirmation Setting

Each lesson includes an affirmation to guide your practice. Embrace these intentions, adjusting them as needed to align with your unique path. They can help you stay focused and open, even when practicing alone. Trust that Spirit is with you, supporting your journey every step of the way.

Reassurance for Solo Practitioners and Beginners

If you're practicing alone or just starting out, remember that most growth comes through personal work with Spirit. Progress takes time, and moments of doubt are natural. Embrace these as part of your journey. Trust that each exercise strengthens your abilities and deepens your understanding.

Journaling Prompts for Self-Reflection

As you practice, reflect on the emotions and sensations that arise. Use prompts like:

- What emotions arise during my practice?
- What signs or sensations am I noticing from Spirit?
- How has my understanding or confidence grown this week?
- What part of my practice felt most meaningful or surprising this week?
- In what ways am I learning to trust my unique way of connecting with Spirit?

These prompts will help you track your experiences, build confidence, and maintain a record of your growth over time.

Instructions for Individual Use

This Guidebook is designed to enhance your personal journey in mediumship, whether you're working on your own or participating in a development circle. Each lesson provides practical exercises, journal prompts, and reflective activities to help you deepen your connection with spirit and develop your abilities at your own pace. What most people do not tell you when you start to develop is that the majority of your work is on you.

You really get out of it what you put in.

How to Use This Guidebook:

- **Weekly Structure**: Follow the Guidebook lesson by lesson, focusing on the specific topic provided. Take your time with each exercise, allowing space for reflection. If you need to go slower, it is okay to take two weeks on a lesson. A big part of development is sharing and learning from others. You may want to explore on-line or in person options.
- **Journaling**: Use the journal prompts to capture your thoughts, experiences, and insights. This will help you track your progress and recognize patterns in your development.
- **Reflection**: At the end of each week, spend time reflecting on what you've learned and how it applies to your journey. This reflection is crucial for integrating the material into your practice. Use the group discussion questions for additional journal prompts.
- **Revisiting Topics**: Mediumship is a spiral process. Feel free to revisit topics as your abilities and understanding evolve.

Your Journey Ahead

Whether you're leading a circle, participating in one guided by this Guidebook, developing your mediumship within a group, or exploring on your own, this Guidebook is your guide to growth, self-discovery, and spiritual connection. Trust your intuition and give yourself the time to progress at your own pace. This journey isn't about rushing—it's about embracing each step with openness and curiosity.

Mediumship is a personal and ever-evolving process. Your connection with Spirit will deepen as you practice and trust the guidance you receive. Some of your greatest teachers are on the other side, ready to assist you through messages, signs, or subtle nudges. In a circle, your facilitators and fellow participants will support you, answering questions and helping you grow. Ultimately, your pace of development is entirely your own. Take your time, trust the process, and lean into the support available on both sides of the veil.

If you ever feel stuck or unsure, revisit what you've learned. Reflecting on past experiences can reignite your connection and provide clarity. This Guidebook is designed as a resource you can return to for guidance and inspiration, whether practicing with a group or on your own. Today, you may be a participant, but one day you could be the facilitator of your own circle. When that time comes, you'll have everything you need to lead with confidence and purpose.

For Experienced Circle Leaders

This Guidebook is an invaluable resource to supplement your existing Development Circle. It's designed to help your participants engage in personal work that will support their growth as mediums and enhance the overall experience of the circle. I debated about splitting this into two books. One for leaders and scaled down guidebook. Yes your participants have a lot of information if you choose to have them work with this guidebook, but it is your experience that will make your development circle come alive for your participants.

Running circles as I have, I was always looking for new meditations, exercises to do with the group, journal prompts, different ways to explain things and there was little out there. I hope that this will add to your already amazing resource library.

If your participants have this Guidebook, you can assign different aspects to augment what you are already doing in your circles.

How to Use This Guidebook:

- **Weekly Integration**: Align the Guidebook's weekly topics with your circle's sessions. Use the exercises, discussions, and journal prompts to deepen participants' understanding and engagement with the material.
- **Facilitation Tips**: Encourage your participants to complete the exercises and journaling outside of circle meetings. During the circle, facilitate discussions based on their experiences and insights.
- **Personal Development:** Emphasize the importance of the personal work each participant does outside the circle. This is where they will internalize the lessons and grow as mediums.
- **Flexibility:** Adapt the Guidebook's material to suit the specific needs and dynamics of your circle. It's designed to be flexible and to complement your existing methods. You may wish to cover in a different order.
- **Other Variations:** You may want to use this book to create a six-week circle as an instructor and not have participants purchase the book. Or you might want to teach a single segment for a specific purpose.

By incorporating this Guidebook into your circle, you're providing a structured yet adaptable framework that supports your participants' ongoing development and strengthens the circle's collective energy.

Instructions for Self-Guided Circles Without a Leader

This Guidebook serves as a guide for creating and running a Mediumship Development Circle, even if your group doesn't have an experienced leader. It's designed to help your group collaborate, enhance your mediumship abilities, and foster a supportive environment for growth.

Rotate leadership responsibilities among members, allowing each person to facilitate a week. While this may feel uncomfortable at first, the experience will strengthen your confidence and group cohesion. Be flexible—if your group needs more time with a topic, take two weeks (or more) to complete it. Move at a pace that feels right for everyone.

How to Use This Guidebook
- **Group Structure:** Establish a regular meeting schedule and decide which member will facilitate each session. The Guidebook's weekly topics provide a clear framework for your meetings.
- **Shared Leadership:** Rotate facilitation to ensure everyone has the chance to lead. This approach builds leadership skills and prevents any one person from feeling overburdened.
- **Group Discussions:** Use the quizzes, discussion questions, and exercises in each lesson to guide your sessions. Encourage open dialogue and the sharing of personal experiences.
- **Personal Work:** Encourage members to complete journal prompts and exercises individually between meetings. Personal reflection is vital to both individual and group growth.
- **Supportive Environment:** Create a non-judgmental space where all members feel safe to explore their abilities and express themselves freely.

By working together, your group can build a strong, cohesive circle.

Starting from Scratch: Insights and Advice

Launching a Development Circle is both exciting and challenging. Whether your group meets in a church, home, or online, the journey is one of learning, adapting, and growing together.

Finding the Right Structure

Early on, I struggled with how to structure the circle. Should it be a fixed number of weeks or ongoing? Over time, I discovered that the 12-week cycle outlined in this Guidebook, followed by a week of reflection, works best. Returning to this cycle helps participants deepen their understanding as new insights emerge each time.

Choosing Activities

Selecting meditations, exercises, and discussion topics can feel daunting. I leaned on activities I'd experienced in other circles, then adapted them to fit my group's needs. Flexibility and openness to change are essential.

Continuing the Journey

Once the 13-week cycle ends, your group can revisit topics as needed or explore alternative topics, try fresh exercises, or explore the journal prompts at the back of this Guidebook. Additional resources are also provided to help maintain momentum.

What continually amazes me is how much I learn as a facilitator. Each circle brings new insights—reminding me that facilitation is a journey of growth as much as participation.

Building a Core Group
- For me, the initial core group came from my church community, which provided a strong foundation. When I moved online, advertising and word of mouth were key in attracting participants. Don't be discouraged if your group starts small—what matters is the commitment and energy each member brings.
- Building trust within the group is crucial, especially when members are just getting to know each other. One practice that worked well for me was having participants send healing to someone at the beginning of the week and then stating three things they were grateful for. This simple exercise helped create a sense of connection and mutual support right from the start.

Maintaining Momentum
- In the early days, I found it challenging to keep the group's momentum going. Without a clear plan, it was easy to lose focus. Once I started bringing handouts, agendas, and information about specific topics, the sessions became more structured and engaging. Having a plan not only gave me confidence as a facilitator but also helped participants feel more grounded in their learning.
- Group dynamics will inevitably change over time. You might encounter a heckler, a skeptic, or someone who struggles with social cues. Learning to navigate these dynamics with patience and flexibility is key. My more experienced members know when I acknowledge the person we are having an issue with and immediately call upon them and as *"So what do you think about what (name of person) said?"* it means I want to move on and need a quick answer.
- As the group matures, offering members the chance to take on the facilitator role can be a powerful teaching moment, helping them build leadership skills and deepen their connection to the material. You can even start with having members be responsible to lead a section of the circle like opening/closing prayers.
- Consistency is the cornerstone of sustaining a Development Circle over the long term. Once you establish a routine that works for your group, stick with it. As the group evolves, continue to introduce new elements or rotate responsibilities to keep things fresh and engaging.
- Setbacks are inevitable, and the COVID-19 pandemic was a major one for many circles. Moving online was challenging and reinforced how much easier it is for some learners to engage in person. However, being adaptable and willing to shift your approach is essential for keeping the circle alive during tough times.

Personal Growth as a Facilitator
- Facilitating a Development Circle has profoundly impacted my personal growth. It has reinforced my connection to spirit and strengthened my understanding of mediumship. Sometimes, the best way to solidify your knowledge is to teach it to others. One key insight I've gained is that I can't be the right facilitator for everyone, and that's okay. Each person's path is unique, and sometimes they'll need to find a different guide who resonates with them.
- Regular feedback from the group is invaluable. It's why I now provide a weekly journal prompt to encourage participants to reflect and write. Many people struggle with knowing what to journal about, so offering a prompt can make a big difference in their personal development.

Key Advice for Starting

My best advice for anyone starting a Development Circle or independent study is simple: just begin. Don't wait for a perfect moment — or you will never begin.

It doesn't have to be perfect, and you can make changes as you go. The most important thing is to start and allow the circle to evolve naturally. Trust the process, and know that you'll grow alongside your participants.

Support Within the Spiritual Community

Mediumship is a deeply personal journey, yet it flourishes within a supportive community. Engaging with others on this path — whether through small, intimate circles or broader networks — creates an invaluable foundation for growth. Within a spiritual community, each person's unique experiences, questions, and insights enrich the group, fostering a sense of belonging and shared purpose.

For those working in circles, the bonds you form with like-minded individuals provide encouragement, feedback, and a safe space to develop your intuitive gifts. The community setting allows you to practice your skills, share experiences, and learn from the insights of others. These shared moments not only strengthen your abilities but also remind you that you're never truly walking this path alone.

Creating Connection Beyond the Circle

If you're practicing solo, remember that you're still part of a larger spiritual community. Visualize yourself connected to others on similar journeys, and know that your experiences and growth contribute to a collective energy of spiritual development. Consider joining online forums, social media groups, or virtual circles to connect with others and share your progress, questions, and breakthroughs.

Nurturing a Circle of Trust and Mutual Support

In any circle, it's essential to create a space of trust, respect, and support. Approach each gathering with an open heart and a commitment to listening as well as sharing. Each member's journey is unique, and their perspectives offer valuable insights. Together, the group's shared energy enhances each person's development, creating a cycle of learning and growth that benefits everyone involved.

Encouragement for Solo Practitioners

If you don't have access to a circle, let this Guidebook and your connection to Spirit serve as a supportive foundation. Trust that your growth is part of a larger wave of spiritual awakening, and that your personal insights resonate beyond your solo practice. By setting an intention to connect with others energetically, you can feel a sense of belonging to a vast and compassionate community of practitioners.

In every step of this journey, remember that spiritual growth is a collective endeavor, enriched by the support and wisdom of others. Whether you're actively engaging in a circle or cultivating a "circle of one," your journey is deeply valued within the spiritual community, and you contribute to its unfolding in meaningful ways.

Notes

Development Lessons

How to Use the Lessons

Each lesson in this Guidebook focuses on a specific topic to support your growth as a spiritual practitioner. While the sequence provided offers a solid foundation, remember: spiritual development isn't linear — it's a spiral. You may find yourself drawn to explore lessons out of order, and that's perfectly okay. Follow the rhythm that feels right for you or your circle.

These lessons were originally designed as weekly topics. Over time, I realized that some people need to linger with certain themes, while others move more quickly. For that reason, I've removed the rigid weekly structure. Take the time you need. Let Spirit — and your own experience — set the pace.

Each lesson begins with a short quiz — not to test you, but to help you see what you already know. It's a gentle way to build confidence and spark curiosity. From there, you'll find an affirmation to center your energy, key concepts to anchor your understanding, and discussion questions to encourage exploration. Select one or two questions, don't feel they all have to be covered or you will not have time to practice. There are also self-reflection questions for each lesson — there are no right or wrong answers. Just you understanding where you are at that moment.

You'll also find both group-based and individual exercises, offering practical ways to work with the material whether you're in a circle or flying solo. Journal prompts are included to guide your self-reflection and deepen your integration.

Once you've moved through all the lessons, don't be surprised if you feel called to circle back. Revisiting the material — especially after you've grown through practice — often reveals deeper meaning and new insights. Each return offers fresh understanding, because you are not the same as when you began.

At the end of this Guidebook, you'll also find:

- Two bonus 30-day journals (Gratitude and Spirit Awareness)
- Meditations to use within your circle
- Additional journal prompts
- A list of conversation topics for future exploration
- Recommended resources to help fill in the gaps

Lesson 1 opens the path. This is my gift to you — born of hard-won wisdom and a deep desire to share what others tried to keep hidden. I am the teacher I once searched for. May you feel seen, supported, and excited to begin.

Lesson 1 Quiz

These quizzes are your guide to help you understand what you know and do not know about the topic. This is meant to be helpful in group discussion in your circle work.

1. **Which technique is commonly used for grounding?**
   a) Visualizing a tree
   b) Watching TV
   c) Using crystals
   d) Reading a prayer

2. **True/False: Grounding helps you stay present and focused.**

3. **Which of the following is a common sign of needing grounding?**
   a) Feeling light-headed
   b) Feeling overly energized
   c) Feeling disconnected from reality
   d) Feeling sleepy

4. **True/False: Protection practices can involve visualizing a protective light.**

5. **Which crystal is most often used for grounding?**
   a) Pyrite
   b) Rose Quartz
   c) Hematite
   d) Citrine

6. **True/False: Grounding is only necessary when feeling unbalanced.**

7. **What color is commonly associated with protection?**
   a) Red
   b) Blue
   c) White
   d) Green

8. **True/False: Prayers are only effective if spoken aloud.**

9. **A grounding exercise can include:**
   a) Eating a meal
   b) Singing a song on the radio
   c) Walking barefoot on the earth
   d) Reading a book

10. **True/False: Grounding and protection should be practiced regularly.**

Notes

Affirmation

"I am grounded, protected, and connected to the Earth."

Lesson 1
Grounding, Protection, and Prayers

Overview

Opening and closing practices are essential when working with Spirit. Prayers, grounding, and protective techniques create a safe, focused environment for your development. Building a strong connection with your guides enhances your mediumship and ensures you work safely in the higher realms.

Above all, a heart filled with love is your strongest protection, raising your vibration and keeping your work rooted in positivity.

See Page 35 for a diagram of creating your own Open/Closing Prayers.

What Is Grounding?

Grounding is the practice of bringing your energy fully into the present moment and reconnecting with your body and the Earth. It helps you feel stable, centered, and clear—especially during spiritual or energetic work. When you're grounded, you can better manage emotions, receive messages more clearly, and stay in control of your own energy.

Grounding Tips

Grounding is both a physical and energetic reset. These simple practices can help you return to your center before and after spiritual work:

- Breathe with purpose. Focus on slow, steady breaths. Inhale through your nose, hold briefly, exhale through your mouth. Imagine your breath anchoring you into the Earth.
- Touch the Earth. Whether it's standing barefoot on grass, sitting beneath a tree, or placing your hand on a stone—direct contact with nature instantly grounds your energy.
- Use grounding crystals. Carry or hold stones like Red Jasper, Hematite, Smoky Quartz, or Black Obsidian. Let them remind your body and spirit to settle.
- Engage your senses. Use the 5-4-3-2-1 **(see page 80)** method to gently bring your awareness into the present. It's especially helpful if your mind feels scattered or overstimulated.
- Move mindfully. Gentle walking, stretching, or dancing brings your awareness back into your body and releases excess energy.
- Eat something nourishing. Foods like root vegetables, nuts, or warm herbal teas can help anchor your energy, especially after intense sessions.
- Visualize rooting. Picture roots growing from the soles of your feet deep into the Earth. Feel your energy settle downward with each exhale.

What is Protection?

Protection is the intentional act of setting energetic boundaries—before, during, and after spiritual work. It's not about fear; it's about discernment. Just as you wouldn't leave your front door wide open to strangers, you don't want your energetic field open to everything.

Spiritual protection helps you stay clear, centered, and connected to your own truth. It ensures that what you receive during your practice comes from a place of light, love, and higher wisdom. Protection isn't about building walls—it's about knowing what is yours and what is not.

There are many ways to protect your energy—and no single method works for everyone. The key is to find what resonates with you and use it with intention.

Common Practices Include:

- Prayer: A simple, heartfelt prayer asking for guidance and protection is often the most powerful.
- Jewelry or Amulets: Worn close to the body, these can serve as both reminders and energetic shields.
- Crystals and Stones: Everyone connects differently. Find the ones that feel supportive and grounding to you.
    - Common choices include: Black Tourmaline, Jet, Labradorite, Fluorite, Blue Kyanite, Black Obsidian, Spirit Quartz, Citrine, Clear Quartz, Rose Quartz, Moonstone, Hematite, Amethyst, and Fire Agate.
- Smudging, Salt, and Coal: Use sage, palo santo, sea salt, or even a bit of coal to clear and protect your space.

Example Opening/Closing Prayers

Opening Prayer:

As we start today, I want to thank Spirit for providing this opportunity to me and those in this circle. Please surround us in the white light of protection and bring forward only the highest and best for all present. Amen.

Closing Prayer:

We thank you for your guidance today in this loving circle with providing the highest and best for all present. Please send healing to all those in need and more importantly for those that have nobody to pray for them. Amen.

Create Your Own Opening Prayer

Opening:	
Statement of Gratitude:	
Your Ask:	
Closing Statement:	

Example: **Infinite Intelligence**: As we start today, I want to thank Spirit for providing this opportunity to me and those in this circle. **Please surround us in the white light of protection and bring forward only the highest and best for all present.** Amen

Create Your Own Closing Prayer

Opening:	
Statement of Gratitude:	
Your Ask:	
Closing Statement:	

Example: **Creator/Father Mother**: We thank you for this time of sharing and now close our connection to Spirit. **As we leave here, we ask for all the healing energy to be sent to all those in need of healing.** Thank you.

Group Meditation — Facilitator Lead Script

Note to Facilitator — take 15-20 seconds between each bold question.

1. Find a quiet and comfortable place to sit. Ensure your cell phone is off. Close your eyes and start by taking a deep breath in through your nose and exhaling slowly through your mouth. Continue to take deep, calming breaths until you feel yourself becoming very relaxed.

2. Imagine yourself walking down a serene path through a beautiful forest. This forest is a safe and welcoming place where the weather is perfect, and you feel completely at home. Take a moment to scan your body from head to toe. **Do you have anything in your hands? How do you feel right now?** Allow yourself to be fully present in this moment. **What season is it? Is it warm or cold? Is the sun out or is it evening and you are guided by the moonlight? What are you wearing in this moment?**

3. As you continue to walk, pay close attention to your surroundings. **What does the path you're on look and feel like? Are there many tall trees surrounding you? Are they all the same or is there a variety of trees? Do you hear the gentle rustling of leaves or the songs of birds?** Notice the intricate details of your forest environment. **What colors do you see? Are there any specific scents in the air? How wide is the path? Is it smooth or are there lots of rocks?** Are there lots of ups and downs as opposed to being level and easy to walk along?

4. Soon, you come across a stream. Pause to dip your hands into the cool, pure water. **Do you take a refreshing sip or decide not to? Is the water crystal clear or is it murky? How does the stream flow? Is it fast or slow? Is there a lot of water, or just a small flow of water? Looking at the stream, what details can you observe about it? Can you see any wildlife? Are there any flowers or ferns near this stream?** Take a moment to truly savor the experience of being by the stream.

5. As you continue, you arrive at the edge of the forest where a beloved animal friend eagerly awaits your arrival. Reach out and greet this familiar companion with your hand, feeling the connection and warmth between you. **Who is this animal? Do they have a name? Ask if they have a message or a gift for you.** Take time to enjoy the presence of this beautiful creature.

6. When you are ready, begin to bring your awareness back to the present moment. Feel your physical body, your seat, and your feet. Start to take deep breaths once more, gradually transitioning back to the room you are in.

7. When you feel fully present, slowly open your eyes. Adjust to your surroundings, bringing the sense of tranquility and connection with you as you return to your day.

8. Come back to the circle and discuss what people felt, saw or sensed during this meditation.

Discuss the signs and symbolism that everyone felt/saw. Use the questions in the above script to prompt the discussion.

Awareness Check: Grounding, Prayer, and Protection

When I feel ungrounded, I usually:

a) Take a few deep breaths
b) Go outside or touch the earth
c) Reach for a grounding stone
d) Forget what to do in the moment

I think of "protection" as:

a) Keeping my energy clear
b) A habit I haven't built yet
c) Something I use only during readings
d) A spiritual boundary that empowers me

Prayer for me is:

a) A daily practice
b) A comfort in uncertain times
c) Something I'm still figuring out
d) Personal and evolving

I know I'm spiritually grounded when:

a) My mind is clear and focused
b) I feel calm and steady
c) I'm able to stay present in the moment
d) All of the above

Group Discussion Questions

- How do you recognize when you are grounded—and when you are not?
- What does energetic protection feel like to you, and how do you know it's in place?
- How has your relationship with prayer evolved as you've deepened your spiritual work?
- What intention do you bring with you when you enter a Development Circle?
- In what ways does opening and closing with prayer change the energy of the circle?
- Have you ever felt ungrounded or unprotected in spiritual work? What did you learn from that experience? What will you do differently going forward?
- What practices help you return to center when you feel scattered or emotionally vulnerable?

Group Exercise—Partnered Energy Sensing

Participants pair up and take turns sensing each other's energy fields. They practice feeling and describing the energy they perceive around their partner.

Instructions:

- Pair up participants naming them a/b. Group A is the Sitter, Group B does the sensing.
- Set a 2-minute timer and instruct the first group to sense the second group in silence.
- The person sensing the energy describes any impressions, images, or feelings they perceive.
- Switch roles and repeat the exercise.
- After both have had a turn, discuss the experience and provide positive feedback in the circle before closing..

This exercise, like all those in this Guidebook, can be revisited as needed.
Circles often incorporate multiple exercises in each session to suit the participants' needs.
Additional exercises can be found at the back of this book for further practice and variety.

Additional Self-Exploration

Visualization

- Find a comfortable position either sitting or lying down.
- Close your eyes and breathe deeply.
- Visualize a place where you feel safe and relaxed. It could be a beach, forest, or a cozy room.
- Engage Your Senses: Imagine the sounds, smells, and sights of this place.
- Stay for a While: Spend a few minutes in this visualization, allowing yourself to feel fully grounded and relaxed.

Nature Connection

- Go outside and find a quiet, natural place.
- Stand barefoot on the grass or soil.
- Take slow, deep breaths in and out.
- Imagine roots growing from the soles of your feet into the earth.
- Visualize drawing up the earth's energy through your roots, filling your body.

Reflect on a time when you felt particularly grounded or protected. What practices contributed to this feeling, and how can you incorporate them into your daily routine?

Weekly Journal Prompt

This week take time and write each day and answer this question:
Why do I feel called to develop my intuitive gifts?

Monday

Tuesday

Wednesday

Thursday

Friday

Saturday

Sunday

Lesson 1 Quiz Answers: 1. A 2. T 3. C 4. T 5. C 6. F 7. C 8. F 9. C 10. T

**Reflect on how your understanding of this week's topic has grown.
Consider any personal experiences or new realizations.
Write about what surprised you, challenged you,
or what you feel most drawn to explore further.**

Lesson 2 Quiz

These quizzes are your guide to help you understand what you know- and do not know about the topic. This is meant to be helpful in group discussion in your circle work.

1. **Which of the following is a common sign of blocked energy?**

    a) Feeling energetic and lively
    b) Experiencing frequent headaches
    c) Being in a good mood
    d) Having a clear mind

2. **True/False: Visualization is a technique that can help enhance energy flow in the body.**

3. **What is the primary purpose of mindfulness meditation?**

    a) To increase physical strength
    b) To improve concentration and awareness of the present moment
    c) To solve complex problems
    d) To induce deep sleep

4. **True/False: Grounding exercises can help balance your energy.**

5. **Which of these practices can help increase mindfulness?**

    a) Multitasking
    b) Eating while watching TV
    c) Focused breathing exercises
    d) Daydreaming

6. **True/False: Meditation requires a completely silent environment to be effective.**

7. **During meditation, which technique can help maintain focus?**

    a) Constantly changing your position
    b) Repeating a mantra
    c) Thinking about your to-do list
    d) Focusing on external noises

8. **True/False: Being mindful means ignoring your thoughts and feelings.**

9. **What is the benefit of practicing mindful breathing?**

    a) It speeds up the metabolism
    b) It reduces stress and promotes relaxation
    c) It increases appetite
    d) It enhances memory instantly

10. **True/False: Energy work is only beneficial for those who believe in it.**

Notes

Affirmation

"I am at the right time to develop my healing and mediumship skills."

Lesson 2

Energy, Meditation, and Mindfulness

Overview

You are more than a body. You are energy in motion—sensitive, connected, and deeply intuitive. This lesson invites you to explore how that energy flows through you, how it is shaped by your thoughts and awareness, and how it connects you to Spirit.

Many people begin their spiritual journey by looking outside themselves for answers. But the real work begins within. As you become more mindful and centered, your energy shifts. Your connection with Spirit deepens. Meditation becomes not just a tool, but a sacred meeting place—a way to listen rather than reach.

In this lesson, we'll explore the foundational elements that support every spiritual practice: the nature of energy, the power of meditation, and the practice of mindfulness. These are not one-time skills, but lifelong companions. You'll also be introduced to the concept of Spirit Guides—those wise, supportive presences who walk with you and work through you.

Let this be a time to listen inward, slow down, and notice what's already stirring within. The sacred is already present. This lesson will help you recognize it.

What Is Energy?
Energy is the subtle life force that flows through all things. It's not random or accidental—it follows metaphysical principles that govern how it moves and interacts. When you focus and refine your energy, its impact grows stronger. This energy, though divine in origin, is part of the natural world—a higher aspect of reality science is still exploring. It carries healing power that nurtures both body and spirit.

What Is Meditation?
Meditation is a mindful practice that helps you quiet the mind, center your awareness, and deepen your connection to Spirit. Through meditation, you cultivate focus and calm, creating space for healing, insight, and spiritual growth.

What Is Mindfulness?
Mindfulness means being fully present and aware of the moment—your thoughts, feelings, sensations, and surroundings—without judgment. It's a way to stay connected with yourself and Spirit, fostering clarity and balance in your daily life.

Let's Talk about our Spirit Guides

Spirit Guides—sometimes called our Spirit Band or Tribe—are our helpers on the other side. As children, we often recognize them easily; adults may call them "imaginary friends." But as we grow, school and church teachings can distance us from that personal connection with Spirit. Reconnecting isn't always easy. It takes unlearning, deep listening, and trust in your inner voice. Think of it like learning to drive a stick shift after years with an automatic—awkward at first, but deeply empowering once it clicks. Connecting with your guides begins with belief—belief in yourself, your essence, and your soul. Nurturing that belief is deeply personal. For some, it starts by quieting the mind and turning inward. Whether you're on a mountaintop, in a forest, or on your couch, the journey begins where you are. Meditation isn't required, but an honest conversation with your inner self is. Approach it with curiosity, not fear—your soul holds treasures waiting to be discovered. .

Spiritualist teaching says we have 7 guides, who have 7 which means we have a large source of help available to us. Each week you gather in circle you build your relationship with your guides. Here are the things you need to know regarding your Guides:

- Don't go in with an agenda - You know what I mean - "I only want Jesus to be my gate keeper" this is where you need to accept who it is.
- Do have boundaries with Spirit! Ask for the highest and best.
- If you don't know who they are you need to ask and keep asking until you know them
- You will need to remember to sit quietly and listen to Spirit.
- Pay attention to signs and symbols, repeating numbers. They can be ways that Spirit is trying to connect with you.
- Prayers are not always answered in the way we hope - but they are answered. It is our willingness to accept it and move forward. And like Garth Brooks sings "Thank God for Unanswered Prayers"
- The biggest thing is to trust in yourself and your connection with Spirit.
- Remember to keep a list of things you need to know from your guides - why journaling is so important
- The answer may not be immediately apparent, but with time you will come to understand.
- Express gratitude to Spirit with every connection, make sure if you are uncomfortable with something that you ask them to respect your boundaries - even if you have to change them.
- Guide Types
    - Joy Guide, Healing Guide & Animals
    - Gatekeeper/Protector (some see them as two or interchangeable)
    - Doctor/Teacher - Philosophy
    - Doctor/Chemist - Think of anything in the sciences, medicine
    - Ascendent Masters, Angels and Saints
    - Fairies, Elves, and Gnomes

Awareness Check: Energy, Meditation & Mindfulness

When I tune into my energy, I notice:

a) Tension or heaviness in certain areas
b) A natural rhythm or flow
c) Nothing at all (yet!)
d) Shifts depending on who I'm around

Meditation for me feels like:

a) A peaceful daily ritual
b) Something I struggle to stay consistent with
c) A moment to reconnect with Spirit
d) New — I'm still figuring it out

Mindfulness helps me to:

a) Stay grounded and present
b) Respond instead of react
c) Notice how others' energy affects me
d) All of the above

I recognize my Spirit Guides through:

a) A sense of presence or knowing
b) Symbols or repeating signs
c) Messages during meditation or dreams
d) I'm not sure yet — but I'm open

Group Discussion Questions

- What is mindfulness? What is meditation? How are they different?
- How can you be more mindful? How does the energy of other people affect us?
- In what ways do you sense or experience the presence of your Spirit Guides?
- How do you recognize when someone else's energy is influencing your own?
- What does it feel like to be fully present in your body? When was the last time you noticed that?
- How can developing a relationship with your guides support your mindfulness?
- What type of meditation works best for you?

Group Exercise — Mindful Listening Circle

- Have participants remain in the circle after a 5-10 minute meditation to help focus.
- Select one person to speak for a 2 minutes about anything on their mind.
- Encourage the rest of the group to listen attentively without interrupting, focusing on the speaker's words, tone, and emotions.
- After the speaker finishes, take a moment of silence for everyone to reflect on what they heard, and ask each person to write down 2-3 key points.
- Have each member share their key point. Did everyone understand the same key point?
- Repeat with different speakers, allowing everyone a chance to share and listen mindfully.
- At the end, discuss how this exercise went and how participants listening evolved over time.

Additional Self-Exploration

Self-Healing Meditation

- Sit or lie down in a comfortable position.
- **Focus on Your Breath:** Close your eyes and take deep, calming breaths.
- **Scan Your Body:** Mentally scan your body from head to toe, noting any areas of tension or discomfort.
- Place your hands on or near the area needing healing. Visualize a warm, glowing light flowing from your hands into the area.
- **Hold the Energy:** Hold this visualization for several minutes, focusing on the healing energy soothing and repairing the area.
- **Close the Session:** Take a few deep breaths and slowly bring your awareness back to the present moment.

> **In what ways can you incorporate mindfulness more consistently into your daily routine?**

Lesson Journal Prompt

This week take time and write each day and answer this question:
How can I empower myself to embrace my gifts?

Monday

Tuesday

Wednesday

Thursday

Friday

Saturday

Sunday

Lesson 2 Quiz Answers: 1. B 2. T 3. B 4. T 5. C 6. F 7. B 8. F 9. B 10. F

**Reflect on how your understanding of this week's topic has grown.
Consider any personal experiences or new realizations.
Write about what surprised you, challenged you,
or what you feel most drawn to explore further.**

Lesson 3 Quiz

These quizzes are your guide to help you understand what you know and do not know about the topic. This is meant to be helpful in group discussion in your circle work.

1. **True/False:** Grief is a universal and deeply emotional experience.

2. **Which of the following is not a healing modality?**
    a) Reiki
    b) Astrology
    c) Acupuncture
    d) Homeopathy

3. **True/False:** The stages of grief always occur in a linear process.

4. **What stage of grief can include emotional outbursts?**
    a) Acceptance
    b) Denial
    c) Depression
    d) Anger

5. **True/False:** Understanding and empathizing with grief's complexities allows mediums to approach their work with sensitivity and compassion.

6. **Which stage of grief is characterized by profound sadness and hopelessness?**
    a) Anger
    b) Bargaining
    c) Depression
    d) Acceptance

7. **True/False:** Grasping the nuances of grief helps mediums offer comfort and closure.

8. **During which stage of grief might a person make deals or wishes to reverse the loss?**
    a) Denial
    b) Anger
    c) Acceptance
    d) Bargaining

9. **True/False:** By understanding grief, mediums can better serve as conduits for healing.

10. **What is the final stage of grief where one comes to terms with the loss?**
    a) Denial
    b) Bargaining
    c) Acceptance
    d) Anger

Notes

Affirmation

"I honor my grief and give myself the space to heal, knowing that my emotions are valid and I am surrounded by love and support."

Lesson 3

Healing and Mediumship

Overview

All spiritual practitioners are natural healers. Whether we realize it or not, our work with Spirit invites healing into the lives we touch. Healing isn't just a concept—it's an active journey of release, renewal, and reconnection with the truth of who we are.

Spiritual healing draws on divine energy, not personal power. A healer doesn't give their own energy—they serve as a channel for Universal or Source energy to support healing of the mind, body, and spirit. If you find yourself exhausted after a healing session, it may be a sign you're giving from your own reserves rather than channeling from Spirit.

Healing can focus on physical pain, emotional wounds, or simply the weariness of a soul in need of comfort. Prayer is one of the most accessible forms of healing—and it works across belief systems. Faith in the healing process matters more than any specific doctrine.

Importantly, we are not medical professionals. We never diagnose or prescribe. Our sacred role is to walk beside others as they heal, offering spiritual support that complements—not replaces—traditional medical care.

Grief's Role in Healing & Mediumship

Grief is one of the most universal—and complex—human experiences. Many people who seek out mediumship are navigating loss. Others may already be within our circles, quietly carrying their grief as they grow spiritually.

As mediums, it's essential that we recognize and honor the emotional terrain of grief. When we understand its depth and nuance, we can meet others with sensitivity, compassion, and care. Our role isn't to fix grief, but to hold space for healing and offer gentle connection when Spirit allows.

Grief does not follow a straight line. While the five stages of grief—denial, anger, bargaining, depression, and acceptance—are widely recognized, they rarely unfold in order. A person may move between them, repeat them, or experience them all at once.

We must be especially attentive during readings. If you sense someone is in the early, raw stages of grief, it's not only appropriate—it's necessary—to pause the reading. Offer them compassion, and, if possible, refer them to professional grief support. Spirit does not ask us to carry what we're not meant to heal alone.

Mediumship can bring peace and connection, but it is never a replacement for professional care. Knowing when to step back is an act of spiritual maturity and love.

Alternative Healing Modalities

Here is a list of alternative healing modalities, for every one listed there are many others:
- Reiki Healing: A Japanese technique that promotes healing. Practitioners use their hands to channel energy into the patient, activating the body's natural healing processes.
- Crystal Healing: Uses gemstones and crystals to promote physical, emotional, and spiritual healing. Different crystals are believed to have specific healing properties.
- Acupuncture: A traditional Chinese medicine practice that involves inserting thin needles into specific points on the body to balance the body's energy flow and promote healing.
- Aromatherapy: Uses essential oils extracted from plants to improve physical and emotional health. These oils can be inhaled or applied to the skin to stimulate healing responses.
- Sound Healing: Utilizes sound frequencies to restore balance and harmony in the body. This can involve instruments like tuning forks, singing bowls, or even the human voice.
- Herbal Medicine: Involves using plants and plant extracts to treat various health conditions. Herbs are used to support the body's healing processes and improve overall health.
- Homeopathy: A natural form of medicine that uses highly diluted substances to trigger the body's self-healing mechanisms. Practitioners believe that these substances stimulate the body's vital force to restore health.

The Stages of Grief: A Brief Overview

Grief often unfolds in a series of emotional stages, though not in a fixed order or timeline. Understanding these stages can help us better support ourselves and others as we navigate loss:

- Denial: The initial shock or disbelief that makes the loss feel unreal.
- Anger: Feelings of frustration, resentment, or helplessness.
- Bargaining: Attempts to regain control by making deals or hoping for a different outcome.
- Depression: Deep sadness and a sense of overwhelming loss.
- Acceptance: Finding peace with the loss and beginning to adjust to a new reality.

Remember, grief is personal and unique. These stages may be revisited multiple times, or experienced in a different sequence. There is no "right" way to grieve — only your way.

If you find yourself in deep or overwhelming grief, speaking with a qualified professional can offer essential support and guidance on your healing journey. Likewise, if you are delivering a message to someone who is deeply grieving, it's best to gently encourage them to seek help from the appropriate professional.

Awareness Check: Grounding, Prayer, and Protection

When a healer feels drained after a session, it usually means:

a) They've used too much of their own energy
b) They channeled energy perfectly
c) The client didn't need healing
d) The energy source was weak

What is an important practice before beginning a healing session?

a) Grounding and protection
b) Focusing on personal problems
c) Ignoring client boundaries
d) Rushing through the session

When working with grief in mediumship, it is essential to:

a) Diagnose the person's emotional state
b) Offer professional therapy
c) Recognize your role and refer when needed
d) Avoid addressing grief

Healing energy flows best when the healer:

a) Is centered and connected to Spirit
b) Is tired and distracted
c) Is focused on their own energy
d) Has little preparation

Group Discussion Questions

- How do you understand the role of hands-on healing in mediumship?
- Do you believe all mediums are natural healers? Why or why not?
- What experiences have you had with healing energy—either giving or receiving it?
- How can healing support the medium's own spiritual growth?
- How do you balance healing work with mediumship abilities in your practice?
- What are some challenges you might face when offering healing through mediumship?
- How do you prepare yourself energetically and emotionally before healing sessions?
- How can understanding grief deepen your healing practice as a medium?

Group Exercise – Practice Hands On Healing

Today you are going to practice hands on healing on one another as well as group healing and distance healing after meditation.

Note You may be required to follow specific protocols for this please refer to your specific church guidelines.

Prayer for Healing (NSAC)

I ask the Great Unseen Healing Force to remove all obstructions from my mind and body
And to restore me to perfect health. I ask this in all sincerity and honesty and I will do my part.
I ask this Great Unseen Healing Force to help both
present and absent ones who are in need of help
And to restore them to perfect health.
I put my trust in the love and power of God.

Additional Self-Exploration

__Journaling Your Grief Journey__

- Daily Reflection: Set aside 10-15 minutes each day to write in a journal. Reflect on your feelings, thoughts, and experiences related to your grief.
- Identify Stages: Note any stages of grief you might be experiencing (Denial, Anger, Bargaining, Depression, Acceptance). Write about how these stages manifest in your daily life.
- Express Emotions: Allow yourself to express all emotions freely. Write about any anger, sadness, confusion, or moments of peace you encounter.
- Review Progress: At the end of each week, review your entries. Notice any patterns or changes in your emotional state and reflect on your progress.
- Not actively grieving? Consider a time when you were in a stage of grief. Or think of a loved one who experienced grief and reflect on what you observed.
- What if you are in the denial stage of grief?

Stop Saying These Phrases

When you are doing healing work (this includes mediumship), remove these phrases from your vocabulary because they sound like a good idea, but they can trigger someone deeply:

There is a reason for everything
You shouldn't feel that way
God needed them more
They are in a better place
It is part of a greater plan
At least…

In what ways can you incorporate healing more consistently into your daily routine?

Weekly Journal Prompt

This week take time and write each day and answer this question:
Write about a sign you received from Spirit each day. How did it make you feel when you got it? What might you do to encourage more signs from Spirit?.

Monday

Tuesday

Wednesday

Thursday

Friday

Saturday

Sunday

Lesson 3 Quiz Answers: 1.T 2. B 3. F 4. B 5. T 6. C 7. T 8. D 9. T 10. C

**Reflect on how your understanding of this week's topic has grown.
Consider any personal experiences or new realizations.
Write about what surprised you, challenged you,
or what you feel most drawn to explore further.**

Lesson 4 Quiz

These quizzes are your guide to help you understand what you know and do not know about the topic. This is meant to be helpful in group discussion in your circle work.

1. **Which part of the brain is typically associated with creativity and intuition?**
    a) left brain
    b) right brain
    c) both equally
    d) neither

2. **True/False:** Building trust with Spirit requires consistent practice and patience.

3. **What is one method to strengthen your intuition?**
    a) meditation
    b) ignoring your inner voice
    c) overthinking every decision
    d) avoiding meditation

4. **True/False:** The left brain is primarily responsible for analytical and logical thinking.

5. **Which activity can help balance the right and left brain dynamics?**
    a) only focusing on logic puzzles
    b) Practicing both analytical and creative exercises regularly
    c) avoiding any mental challenges
    d) focusing only on physical activities

6. **True/False:** Trusting your intuition can enhance your mediumship abilities.

7. **How can you build trust with Spirit?**
    a) by doubting every sign
    b) by not practicing regularly
    c) by disregarding any messages you receive
    d) by setting intentions and being open to receiving

8. **True/False:** Intuition can be developed through regular practice and awareness.

9. **Which brain hemisphere is more involved in tasks requiring spatial awareness and holistic thinking?**
    a) left brain
    b) right brain
    c) neither
    d) both equally

10. **True/False:** Developing your intuition is an instant process that requires no effort.

Notes

Affirmation

"I express my intuitive insights with clarity and confidence."

Lesson 4
Trusting Your Intuition
Overview

We'll explore the "clairs" later. For now, let's focus on intuition—your soul's compass. It speaks through dreams, empathy, gut feelings, or a sudden shift in thought when Spirit is near. Many ask, "Is this just my imagination?" That first feeling, image, or word? That's the doorway. Trust it before doubt creeps in.

As children, we trusted this inner knowing. But over time, we're taught to favor logic and quiet the soul's voice. True growth means honoring both. Trusting intuition is really remembering what you've always known—you can connect with divine wisdom.

Imagination envisions what hasn't happened yet.

Intuition knows without needing to explain.

Both are gifts—but intuition is Spirit's calling card. The more you trust it, the louder it becomes.

Left/Right Brain

Knowing each side's strength, you can leverage for better messages.
> The left brain is logical and handles reading, writing, and calculations.
> The right brain is more visual and deals in images more than words.

How do you build trust with Spirit?

Building trust with Spirit is a personal journey. Others can offer techniques, but true trust comes from your own lived experience—just like any meaningful relationship.

Here are some essentials to help you develop that trust:
- Pay attention to the details. Spirit often speaks in subtle ways.
- Believe in yourself—and be patient. Confidence builds over time.
- Allow yourself to be wrong. Mistakes are part of learning.
- In a reading or greeting, give the symbol—don't interpret it first. Let the recipient find its meaning.
- It's not your message. One of the hardest (but most freeing) things is to stop trying to make sense of what you receive. Just share it.
- Stop discounting your experiences. Trust what you're getting.
- Trust Spirit to honor your boundaries. You're not alone in this work.

The more you show up with honesty and consistency, the more trust will grow—on both sides of the veil.

Setting Your Intentions

Before any meaningful practice — whether it's meditation, healing, or connection with Spirit — pause and ask yourself: What am I here for? Setting an intention grounds your energy and gives your practice direction. It's not about forcing an outcome; it's about aligning with your soul's truth.

- Intentions are more than wishes. They are quiet declarations to the Universe about how you want to show up in this moment. When you name them with clarity and trust, Spirit responds. Intention is the soul's compass — it keeps you aligned, centered, and open.
- Get clear on where you want to go and set it. Your intention will keep you on track.
- An intention is a guiding principle for how you want to be, live, and show up in the world — during meditation, yoga or any area of your life.
- The best time to plant your intentions is during the period after meditation, while your awareness remains centered in the quiet field of all possibilities. After you set an intention, let it go — simply stop thinking about it. Continue this process daily until it becomes a habit.

The Power of Patience

Patience is not just waiting — it's a loving act of faith in your spiritual journey. Sometimes, Spirit's timing feels slow or even invisible. When you notice others seeming to grasp things quickly, it's easy to feel discouraged or doubt yourself. But remember, your path is unique, and growth cannot be rushed. Comparing yourself to others only dims your own light. Instead, be gentle with yourself. Trust that your intuition is unfolding exactly as it should, even if you can't see the full picture yet.

Consider the growth of the fern and the bamboo. The fern sprouts and unfurls quietly, day by day, steadily growing in its own time. Bamboo, on the other hand, spends years growing roots beneath the surface before it shoots up rapidly, towering overnight. Your spiritual growth works the same way — sometimes visible and steady like the fern, sometimes unseen and deep like the bamboo's roots. Both are necessary and beautiful.

Often, the deepest messages come in moments of quiet stillness, when you least expect them. These pauses are sacred spaces where Spirit quietly works beneath the surface. Embrace the unknown with kindness, knowing each small step forward builds your faith and strengthens your connection. Keep showing up with patience and an open heart. Your willingness to trust — even in the waiting — is the very foundation of your spiritual growth. Your time is coming, and Spirit is with you every step of the way.

Awareness Check: Trusting Your Intuition

Natural Law is best described as:

a) A set of universal, inherent principles
b) Rules created by religious leaders
c) Guidelines only for mediums
d) A modern concept with little spiritual relevance

My intuition most often speaks to me through:

a) Dreams or inner visions
b) Sudden feelings or "gut" instincts
c) A quiet inner knowing
d) All of the above

The biggest block to trusting Spirit is often:

a) Not enough training
b) A lack of imagination
c) Fear of being wrong
d) Too many spirit guides

A helpful way to build trust in Spirit is to:

a) Keep a journal of intuitive hits
b) Seek external validation constantly
c) Compare myself to other mediums
d) Only practice when I feel 100% confident

Group Discussion Question

- How do you know when you're receiving intuitive guidance versus overthinking?
- What helps you build trust with Spirit, especially when doubt creeps in?
- Can you share a time when following your intuition made a difference?
- How does fear of being wrong impact your ability to trust what you receive?
- In what ways does trusting Natural Law support your spiritual practice?
- How does understanding that "truth is simple" influence your readings or healing work?
- What's one practice that helps you reconnect with your intuitive self when you feel blocked?

Group Exercise — Intuitive Drawing

Materials Needed: Blank paper, colored pencils or crayons.

- Sit in a circle and give each participant a sheet of blank paper and colored pencils or crayons.
- Ask everyone to close their eyes and take a few deep breaths to center themselves.
- Guide them to focus on a question or intention related to their mediumship journey.
- With eyes closed or slightly open, allow the participants to draw or doodle whatever comes to their mind, without overthinking.
- After 5-10 minutes, invite everyone to share their drawings and discuss any insights or feelings that arose during the exercise. Does anyone one else's drawing feel like a message to you?

Additional Self-Exploration

Visualization Practice

Instructions:
- Spend 5-10 minutes each day visualizing a peaceful scene or an encounter with a guide or Spirit.
- Focus on the details and sensations, allowing the visualization to become vivid.
- Note any messages or feelings you receive during these sessions.

Symbol Interpretation

- Select a symbol (e.g., a feather, a key, a heart) and meditate on its meaning for you.
- Throughout the week, notice when and where this symbol appears in your life.
- Record these occurrences and your interpretation of their significance in your journal.

> Stop scrutinizing what is missing and start scrutinizing the subtle experiences that are happening for you! With that above, In addition to the weekly prompt, start journaling and paying attention to what is happening around you. Consciously decide each day how you wish to honor your Spirit. Journal about what you have perceived, lesson(s) that were meant for you and what your soul and Spirit are trying to communicate with you.

Weekly Journal Prompt

This week take time and write each day and answer this question:
Pay attention each day to how you are aware of Spirit's presence, write about each experience. Do you see any trends?

Monday

Tuesday

Wednesday

Thursday

Friday

Saturday

Sunday

Lesson 4 Quiz Answers: 1. B 2. T 3. A 4. T 5. B 6. T 7. D 8. T 9. B 10. F

**Reflect on how your understanding of this week's topic has grown.
Consider any personal experiences or new realizations.
Write about what surprised you, challenged you,
or what you feel most drawn to explore further.**

Lesson 5 Quiz

These quizzes are your guide to help you understand what you know and do not know about the topic. This is meant to be helpful in group discussion in your circle work.

1. **True/False**: Signs and symbols can be unique to each individual.

2. **Signs from spirit often come in the form of:**
    a) Numbers
    b) Dreams
    c) Animals
    d) All of the above

3. **True/False:** Trusting your intuition is not necessary to interpret signs from spirit.

4. **A common way to receive symbols is through:**
    a) Meditation
    b) Watching TV
    c) Reading books
    d) Listening to music

5. **True/False:** Interpreting signs requires you to analyze them logically.

6. **Which of the following can be considered a sign from spirit?**
    a) A specific song playing repeatedly
    b) A recurring thought or feeling
    c) A feather appearing in unexpected places
    d) All of the above

7. **True/False:** Spirit will only use symbols you already understand.

8. **Trusting your intuition can help you:**
    a) Understand messages from spirit
    b) Develop your mediumship skills
    c) Build confidence in your abilities
    d) All of the above

9. **True/False:** Signs and symbols are always clear and easy to interpret.

10. **When you notice a sign, it is important to:**
    a) Ignore it
    b) Reflect on its meaning
    c) Share it with others immediately
    d) Write it down

Notes

Affirmation

"My intuition is strong, and I see the signs and symbols from Spirit with clarity."

Lesson 5

Signs and Symbols

Overview

Spirit speaks in many languages—and one of the most common is symbolism. Symbols show up in dreams, during readings, and even in your day-to-day life. They are Spirit's shorthand—a meaningful way to get your attention.

But here's the key: symbols are deeply personal. While some meanings are commonly shared, others are unique to you. A butterfly may signal transformation to one person and a specific loved one to another. That's why it's so important to share and discuss symbols within your circle.

Start building your personal symbol dictionary. Keep a journal. Track dreams. Reflect on colors, animals, numbers, sounds, and even wordplay—Spirit loves puns! Over time, you'll begin to recognize patterns and grow more confident in the messages.

Eventually, you won't need to log every sign. You'll simply know when Spirit is nudging you—and what they mean by it.

Dreams

During the day, our conscious mind is busy with logic and decisions. But at night, that part of us rests—allowing the subconscious to rise and speak. Spirit often uses this quiet space to send insight, healing, or even visitations. Our dreams become a meeting place for soul work and subtle guidance.

Symbols frequently appear in dreams. These may be animals, colors, numbers, people, or scenes that feel significant. Some symbols are universal, while others are deeply personal. Trust your intuition as you reflect on them. What something means to you matters more than what a book might say.

Keeping a dream journal can help you deepen this practice. Place a notebook and pen by your bed. Write down anything you recall as soon as you wake—images, feelings, snippets of dialogue. Dreams fade quickly, so capture them before you do anything else.

This takes practice, like any spiritual discipline. Over time, your recall improves and meaningful patterns emerge. You'll begin to recognize when your subconscious—and Spirit—are speaking through symbol and story.

Before sleep, take a moment to set the intention to remember your dreams. Picture yourself waking and writing them down. Hold that image in your mind as you drift off. This helps imprint the practice and invites Spirit to meet you in the dream space.

Animal Guides: Messengers from Spirit

Animals are powerful messengers, often appearing in our lives—awake or asleep—with meaning and guidance. In many traditions, they are considered spirit allies or totems, helping us navigate our spiritual path.

An animal may show up repeatedly in dreams, on your walks, in art, or through conversation. Pay attention to these moments. They're rarely coincidence. Spirit may be sending you a nudge.

Each animal carries its own energetic message:

- Hawk may ask you to rise above and see the bigger picture.
- Butterfly could signal a time of transformation.
- Wolf may be reminding you to honor your instincts and pack.
- Deer might be asking for gentle strength and sensitivity.

But remember—your relationship to the symbol matters most. A crow may mean mystery and magic to one person and comfort and protection to another. There's no one-size-fits-all definition when it comes to Spirit.

You don't need to memorize meanings. Simply begin to notice. Keep a record in your journal of the animals you encounter and how you feel when they appear. Ask Spirit what message is meant for you. Then be still and open to the response.

Animal guides offer us grounding, wisdom, and support. Let them walk with you.

Understand Relationships

Relationships can be easy – Mother/Father, Brother/Sister, Friend, Teacher/Student

Mother for example, may have multiple meanings: Mother: some people have Grandmothers and Great grandmothers, Godmothers, Mother-in-laws, Foster Moms, Step Moms, Work Moms, Aunts/Grandmothers that take the role of Mother, a friend's mother who treats you like a daughter. There are multiple names that could be used: Mama, Mom, Mommy, Ma, Mother.

This is why it's vital to know how you define your relationships. Spirit often speaks through your frame of reference. When you're clear about the roles people have played in your life, you'll better recognize the connections Spirit is highlighting. It's not always about a biological link—it's about the bond, the feeling, the role they held in your heart.

You've reflected on what 'Mother' means to you—now pause and consider: what comes up when you hear 'Father'... or 'Friend'... or 'Sister'?

Awareness Check: Signs & Symbols

Journaling signs and dreams helps me:

a) See patterns over time
b) b) Deepen my connection to Spirit
c) c) Strengthen my interpretation skills
d) d) All of the above

I can tell a dream is spiritually significant when:

a) It feels different or vivid
b) b) It stays with me after waking
c) c) It carries emotion or clarity
d) d) Any of the above

Spirit might use numbers, colors, animals, flowers, objects or songs as:

a) Entertainment
b) Distractions
c) Symbols
d) Confusion

I know I've received a sign when:

a) I feel a deep inner knowing
b) It confirms something I asked about
c) I sense peace or clarity
d) All of the above

Group Discussion Questions

- What are the top 3 signs you're seeing, hearing, or sensing right now?
- Can one symbol or sign have different meanings for different people? Share an example.
- How do signs show up for you — through feelings, tastes, smells, music, or something else?
- Have you ever dismissed a sign, only to realize its meaning later? What happened?
- What was your sign or nudge to join a Development Circle?
- Do you have a lucky number, animal, or recurring image? Where do you think it came from?
- How do your dreams communicate with you? Share a symbol or theme that repeats for you.

Group Exercise — Partner Reading

- Pair up the participants. Each pair sits facing each other and takes a few moments to center themselves with deep breathing. One partner closes their eyes and focuses on receiving intuitive messages or symbols for their partner.
- The person with closed eyes shares any images, feelings, or symbols that come to mind without filtering or overthinking.
- The receiving partner provides feedback on how these messages resonate with their current life situation or spiritual journey.
- Switch roles and repeat the process.
- After both partners have shared, discuss as a group the different symbols and messages received, highlighting the importance of trusting one's intuition.

Additional Self-Exploration

Symbol Research

Objective: Expand your knowledge of common spiritual symbols and their meanings.

Instructions:

Choose a symbol that you encounter frequently or feel drawn to. Research its historical, cultural, and spiritual meanings. Reflect on how these meanings resonate with your personal experiences and spiritual journey. Write a short essay or journal entry about your findings and personal reflections.

Nature Walk for Symbol Discovery

Objective: Connect with nature to receive signs and symbols from the natural world.

Instructions:

Go for a walk in nature, such as a park, forest, or beach. Set the intention to be open to receiving signs and symbols from Spirit. Pay close attention to the sights, sounds, and sensations around you. Take note of any symbols or signs that stand out to you, such as specific animals, plants, or natural formations. Reflect on the meanings of these symbols and how they relate to your current life circumstances. Write about your experience and insights in your journal.

Reflect on any patterns or synchronicities you have noticed in your life recently. How do these patterns connect to your current life situation or spiritual path? Consider the possible messages or guidance these synchronicities are offering you. How can you apply these insights to enhance your personal growth and your connection with Spirit?

Weekly Journal Prompt

This week take time and write each day and answer this question:
**Reflect on the signs and symbols you encounter.
Write about their meanings and how they make you feel.
How do these experiences strengthen your intuition and trust with Spirit? Any patterns?**

Monday

Tuesday

Wednesday

Thursday

Friday

Saturday

Sunday

Lesson 5 Quiz Answers: 1. T 2. D 3. F 4. A 5. F 6. D 7. F 8. D 9. F 10. B

**Reflect on how your understanding of this week's topic has grown.
Consider any personal experiences or new realizations.
Write about what surprised you, challenged you,
or what you feel most drawn to explore further.**

Lesson 6 Quiz

These quizzes are your guide to help you understand what you know and do not know about the topic. This is meant to be helpful in group discussion in your circle work.

1. **True/False**: Clairvoyance means clear seeing.

2. **Which clair refers to clear hearing?**
    a) Clairaudience
    b) Clairvoyance
    c) Clairsentience
    d) Claircognizance

3. **True/False**: Clairsentience involves clear feeling.

4. **What practice can help develop clairvoyance?**
    a) Visualization
    b) Meditation
    c) Prayer
    d) All of the above

5. **True/False**: Claircognizance means clear knowing.

6. **What does clairalience refer to?**
    a) Smelling
    b) Tasting
    c) Knowing
    d) Hearing

7. **True/False**: Clairalience involves clear smelling.

8. **Clairgustance refers to which sense?**
    a) Hearing
    b) Seeing
    c) Feeling
    d) None of the above

9. **True/False**: You can develop a sense that you are currently not using with practice

10. **What can enhance the development of the clairs?**
    a) Journaling
    b) Reflecting on experiences
    c) Practicing daily
    d) All of the above

Notes

Affirmation

"I am grounded and aware of the subtle signs Spirit shares."

Lesson 6
Using Your Senses
Overview

In this lesson, we explore the fascinating world of the clairs—the intuitive senses through which Spirit communicates. These abilities can deepen your connection with Spirit and enhance your practice, whether you're working psychically, as a medium, or as a healer. Each clair links to different chakras and aspects of your energetic system, helping you tune in with more clarity and ease.

As you develop, Spirit may work through any or all of your senses. You might receive messages as inner visuals, subtle sounds, emotions, or physical sensations. Sometimes it's a quiet knowing, a shift in energy, or even a symbolic taste or smell. While Lesson 5 focused on signs and symbols, this lesson helps you identify how those messages are received—and what senses are at play when Spirit communicates.

These messages may also surface in dreams or through the imagination. Don't dismiss them— Spirit often works through what is familiar and accessible to you.

It's also normal to become more sensitive during development. You may feel a bit overwhelmed at times, especially as your awareness sharpens. The good news? It gets easier. Your body, mind, and energy field will adjust.

Most importantly, you are always in charge of your spiritual experience. If a certain sensation or form of communication feels uncomfortable, you can ask Spirit not to use that method. Development should feel empowering, safe, and aligned with your needs.

Now, let's take a closer look at each of the clairs—and discover how they might already be showing up in your life.

Spirit Communication is Vast

In the physical world we receive information in many ways. For example, if someone wanted to invite you to a party they could they could tell you in person, call, text, send a formal invitation or even post it on Facebook. Spirit can't use these methods to communicate so it uses:

- Signs and Symbols
- Dreams & Imagination
- Clairaudience - Hearing
- Clairessence - Smell
- Clairgustience – Taste
- Claircognizance – clear knowing
    - Intuition, Instinct
- Clairsentience - feeling
    - Empathy
    - Psychometry
- Clairvoyance (ESP) - seeing
    - Precognition **(see Page 123)**
    - Remote Viewing
    - Telepathy

Definitions

Psychometry—The ability to receive intuitive or spiritual information by touching an object. The item often holds energy or memories, and by holding it, a person may sense its history or the emotions of those connected to it.

Precognition—The ability to sense or know something before it happens. This may come through dreams, sudden insight, or intuitive nudges that later prove true.

Remote Viewing—The practice of "seeing" or sensing a person, place, or object at a distance without using physical senses. It often involves visual impressions or knowing details about something not physically present.

Telepathy—Mind-to-mind communication—receiving thoughts, emotions, or words from another person without speaking. It can feel like suddenly knowing what someone else is thinking or feeling.

Numeric Meanings in Readings

Numbers are often some of the first signs we notice from Spirit. Repeating numbers catch our attention at first, then appear more frequently—sometimes almost everywhere we look.

You might miss the first few signs, but they grow louder with time and practice, becoming easier to recognize. Like many signs, numbers can have multiple meanings and sometimes cause confusion. If you keep seeing numbers, start writing them down. Look for patterns to help you understand their messages. In readings or messages, numbers can relate to many things, including:

- An address or zip code
- Phone number (whole or part)
- Account Number
- Money
- # of siblings, children
- # of minutes/hours/days/weeks/months
- # of (fill in the blank)
- Birth/Death date
- Anniversary
- Jersey number
- Time (past/present/future)
- Coordinates xxxx
- License Plate
- Numerology (see page 96)
- The number itself could have meaning:
  - 11/11 New Beginnings
- 222 Balance, trust the process
- 000 Unity with the universe
- 1212 Spiritual awakening
- 1010 Personal development
- 1234 Take the helm
- Google "Angel Numbers Joanne Walmsley" for complete list
- It could be someone's life or path number
- It could be an inside joke between the sitter and the Spirit
- The numbers could represent letters of numerology
  - A, J, S = 1; B, K, T = 2; C, L, U = 3; D, M, V = 4; E, N, W = 5; F, O, X = 6; G, P, Y = 7; H, Q, Z = 8; I, R = 9

Awareness Check: The Clairs

I often feel Spirit's presence through:

a) Emotions or energy shifts
b) Inner vision or mental pictures
c) Words, sounds, or music in my mind
d) I haven't noticed Spirit's presence (yet)

Do you ever smell or taste something with no clear source (like perfume, smoke)?

a) Yes, and I often associate it with Spirit or memory
b) Occasionally, but I don't think much about it
c) Rarely, and I tend to dismiss it
d) Never

When I dream, I tend to:

a) Feel emotions strongly, even after waking
b) See vivid imagery or symbolic scenes
c) Hear voices, songs, or spoken guidance
d) Rarely remember my dreams

When I walk into a space, I often notice:

a) The mood or energy of the room
b) Visual details others might overlook
c) A physical reaction in my body (tingles, tension, etc.)
d) Nothing in particular

Group Discussion Questions

- Have any of you noticed recurring patterns or synchronicities in your life? What do you think these patterns are trying to tell you?
- How do your senses (sight, hearing, touch, etc.) help you recognize and interpret signs and symbols from Spirit? Can you share an experience where your senses played a key role?
- Have any of you noticed recurring patterns or synchronicities in your life? What do you think these patterns are trying to tell you?
- How do your senses (sight, hearing, touch, etc.) help you recognize and interpret signs and symbols from Spirit? Can you share an experience where your senses played a key role?
- Which of the clairs do you feel most connected to right now? How has that sense shown up in your spiritual work or daily life?

Group Exercise — Group Symbol Meditation

- The facilitator leads the group in a guided meditation focused on receiving symbols and signs from Spirit. *(See example script on Page 36)*
- Participants sit comfortably in a circle, close their eyes, and take deep breaths to relax.
- During the meditation, the facilitator prompts participants to visualize a specific theme (e.g., protection, guidance, healing) and remain open to receiving any symbols or signs related to this theme.
- After 5-10 minutes, participants open their eyes and write down any symbols, images, or feelings they experienced.
- Each participant then shares their experiences with the group.
- Discuss any common symbols or themes that emerged — reflect on their collective meaning.

Additional Self-Exploration

Strengthening Your Senses

Pay attention to your senses (hearing, seeing, smelling, tasting, and feeling) over the next week. Each day focus on one sense and pay attention.

Feeling adventurous? Try two at a time smelling and tasting are a good combination to start with.

- For hearing – See if you can hear things beyond what you normally hear
- For seeing – look for patterns, colors, and the details of ordinary objects
- For smelling – take in the aroma of things cooking, your coffee or soap when you shower
- For tasting – be aware of the flavors of your food. Try new spices.
- For feeling – run your fingers over different surfaces, not how they feel to you

This practice will help you heighten your awareness and enhance your intuitive abilities. Enjoy the exploration!

> **This week, write about your experiences with your senses. Which sense is strongest for you? Which one makes you feel uncomfortable? Is there a sense you want to grow?**

Weekly Journal Prompt

This week take time and write each day and answer this question:
Reflect on your daily practice with the clairs this week. Which clair felt the strongest or most natural to you? How did you cultivate this ability?

Monday

Tuesday

Wednesday

Thursday

Friday

Saturday

Sunday

Lesson 6 Quiz Answers: 1. T 2. A 3. T 4. D 5. T 6. A 7. F 8. D 9. T 10. D

Additional Self-Exploration

Exercise Your Ability to Hear

I want you to sit with one piece of music that has multiple instruments along with vocals. Listen to it multiple times. Each time I want you to try and follow a different instrument or vocal all the way through the song. This will help you open your mind to listening in a cluttered space. This works well as a group exercise in circle as well. Some songs that may work include:

- Don't Let the Sun Go Down On Me — George Michael/Elton John (Live)
- Daybreak - Barry Manilow
- Layla - Eric Clapton
- Dream On - Aerosmith
- Why - Annie Lennox
- From a Distance - Bette Midler
- Respect - Aretha Franklin
- Saturday in the Park - Chicago
- Scarborough Fair - Sara Brightman's version
- Moondance - Van Morrison
- Hot Blooded - Foreigner
- Complicated - Avril Lavigne
- Imagine - John Lennon
- Girls Just Want to Have Fun - Cyndi Lauper
- Third Eye - Florence & the Machine
- Tusk — Fleetwood Mac
- Simply Irresistible - Robert Palmer

The 5-4-3-2-1 Grounding Technique

Feeling overwhelmed or disconnected? This simple exercise brings you back to the present moment using your five senses. It's a powerful way to reduce anxiety and reset your nervous system — no tools required.

Here's how it works:

5 - Look around and name five things you can see.
Pick out colors, patterns, or tiny details you'd usually overlook.

4 - Notice four things you can feel.
The fabric of your clothes, the ground under your feet, the breeze on your skin.

3 - Listen for three sounds you can hear.
Focus on what's around you: birdsong, a humming appliance, distant voices.

2 - Breathe in and identify two things you can smell.
If you can't smell anything, find a nearby object or move gently to shift your surroundings.

1 - Acknowledge one thing you can taste.
It might be a sip of tea, a mint, or just the taste in your mouth.

This grounding practice reconnects you with your body and your environment. It's especially helpful during moments of stress, emotional overwhelm, or spiritual disconnection.

Tip: Try using this technique at the start of a meditation or circle session to settle your energy.

Six Lesson Review Quiz

1. True/False: Grounding is a technique used to connect with the earth's energy.

2. True/False: Meditation is a practice that helps quiet the mind and enhance focus.

3. True/False: Clairvoyance is the ability to hear messages from spirits.

4. True/False: Healing can occur on physical, emotional, and spiritual levels.

5. True/False: Protection rituals are unnecessary for experienced mediums.

6. True/False: Prayers can be used to set intentions before a mediumship session.

7. True/False: Signs and symbols are often used by spirits to communicate messages.

8. True/False: Mindfulness is about being aware of the present moment without judgment.

9. True/False: Energy work is only beneficial for physical healing.

10. True/False: Developing intuition requires practice and patience.

11. True/False: Clairsentience involves sensing the emotions or physical sensations of spirits.

12. True/False: Building trust with spirit guides can enhance mediumship abilities.

13. True/False: The left brain is associated with creative and intuitive thinking.

14. True/False: Grounding can help prevent feeling overwhelmed during a reading.

15. True/False: Mediumship involves communicating with spirits to deliver messages.

16. True/False: Mediumship is not a form of Healing.

17. True/False: Mindfulness practices can improve a medium's ability to connect with spirit.

18. True/False: Protection techniques are only necessary during group sessions.

19. True/False: Meditation can enhance both energy work and mediumship.

20. True/False: Understanding the clairs can help a medium interpret messages more accurately.

Quiz Answers: 1. T, 2. T, 3. F, 4. T, 5. F, 6. T, 7. T, 8. T, 9. F, 10. T, 11. T, 12. T, 13. F, 14. T, 15. T, 16. F, 17. T, 18. F, 19. T, 20. T

**Reflect on how your understanding of this week's topic has grown.
Consider any personal experiences or new realizations.
Write about what surprised you, challenged you,
or what you feel most drawn to explore further.**

Lesson 7 Quiz

These quizzes are your guide to help you understand what you know and do not know about the topic. This is meant to be helpful in group discussion in your circle work.

1. **True/False:** Spiritual beliefs can shape and enhance mediumship practices.

2. **True/False:** Meditation is not essential for strengthening the connection with spirit.

3. **Which of the following is a spiritual practice that can support mediumship?**
    a) Yoga
    b) Journaling
    c) Prayer
    d) All of the above

4. **True/False:** Sharing your reflections on spirituality with others can hinder your mediumship growth.

5. **Spirituality in mediumship primarily involves:**
    a) Rituals
    b) Personal beliefs
    c) Scientific methods
    d) None of the above

6. **True/False:** Connecting with spirit can deepen your understanding of your spiritual path.

7. **A common spiritual practice for mediums is:**
    a) Watching TV
    b) Praying
    c) Shopping
    d) Sleeping

8. **True/False:** Reflective journaling can help mediums integrate their spiritual experiences.

9. **To enhance mediumship, one should:**
    a) Ignore spiritual practices
    b) Integrate spiritual beliefs
    c) Avoid meditation
    d) None of the above

10. **True/False:** Engaging in nature walks can be a spiritual practice that supports mediumship.

Notes

Affirmation

"I am open to the infinite possibilities of the universe."

Lesson 7

Spirituality and Mediumship

Overview

Spirituality and mediumship are deeply connected—each one enriching the other. Spirituality is a personal journey, a path to connect with something greater than yourself. It nurtures your inner world and brings deeper meaning to your life and your work with Spirit.

Mediumship, at its core, is spiritual work. It involves communicating with those in Spirit, bridging the physical and non-physical realms. But more than that, it's about healing, insight, and transformation. A strong spiritual foundation supports this work—it creates clarity, protection, and guidance.

Unlike religion, which is often based on someone else's experience passed down through structure and tradition, spirituality is your own experience—shaped by what you believe, feel, and know to be true. That's why you won't find dogma here. There's no one right way to believe. What matters is your personal connection to a higher power—whatever that looks like for you.

In this work, I encourage exploration. Learn about mystic and religious experiences from many traditions. See what speaks to you. In circle, we honor the diverse spiritual paths of each participant. There is deep value in learning from one another.

For some, this journey can feel like a spiritual deconstruction. Old beliefs may be challenged. You may feel lost, unsure, or even question everything. That's okay. There is no rush, no pressure. We support one another through listening, honest discussion, and nonjudgmental presence. Growth happens through dialogue.

A consistent spiritual practice—whether it's prayer, meditation, journaling, or quiet reflection—becomes a container for development. These practices help you process what you're learning, integrate what you're receiving, and stay grounded in your own truth. That's why I strongly encourage journaling: it gives you a visual map of where you are and where you've been.

You don't need to be religious to develop spiritually. And you don't need to believe in spirit communication to be welcome here. Everyone is entitled to their own path. Some come to this work to open the door; others come to learn how to close it in a healthy way. Either is valid.

Mediumship is both a calling and a skill. And like any skill, it becomes easier and more joyful when rooted in a spiritually centered life.

What is Natural Law? Why is it so Important?

This may be one of the hardest topics we'll explore together—because it asks us to take radical responsibility for how we move through the world. I'll be honest: I've wrestled with it myself. Understanding Natural Law isn't just an intellectual exercise; it's a spiritual reckoning. It invites us to look at the invisible threads that tie our intentions, actions, and consequences together.

- Natural Law isn't about punishment or reward. It's about alignment—with truth, with love, and with the way Spirit works. It reminds us that our spiritual path isn't random—it's relational. What we send out energetically returns to us. How we show up matters.
- In the work of Mediumship and spiritual development, Natural Law is the unseen current. It carries our messages, shapes our healing, and helps us navigate the sacred responsibility of working with Spirit.

Here are its key truths:

Inherent Truths: These laws aren't created by humans. They're the foundation of the Universe—principles like balance, justice, love, and truth.

Spiritual Integrity: When we align with Natural Law, we honor both Spirit and sitter. We don't manipulate energy—we work with it.

Awareness Is Access: You don't need a theology degree to understand these laws. You already know them. Your soul remembers.

Empowerment Through Responsibility: This path calls us to own our thoughts, energy, and actions. That can feel heavy, but it's also freeing. We're not powerless—we're powerful co-creators. This isn't easy work. But it's sacred work. And you're not doing it alone.

Natural Laws Descriptions

The Law of Vibration: Everything in the universe is in constant motion and has its own frequency.
The Law of Attraction: Our thoughts and energies attract similar energies and experiences.
The Law of Cause and Effect (Karma): Every action has a corresponding reaction that returns to us.
The Law of Compensation: The universe balances energy, rewarding good deeds and correcting negative ones.
The Law of Perpetual Transmutation of Energy: Energy constantly changes forms, and we can transform negative into positive.
The Law of Relativity: Our experiences are influenced by how we compare them to others.
The Law of Polarity: Everything has an opposite, helping us understand balance and harmony.
The Law of Rhythm: Life operates in cycles and recognizing these patterns helps us navigate highs and lows.
The Law of Gender: Everything contains both masculine and feminine energies that need balance.

The Golden Rule: A Universal Truth Rooted in Natural Law

Across every major spiritual tradition, one principle shines through: *treat others as you would wish to be treated.* Known as the Golden Rule, this guiding truth is more than moral advice—it's a reflection of Natural Law, that sacred order woven into the fabric of existence.

The Essence of the Golden Rule

At its heart, the Golden Rule is a call to empathy. Whether phrased positively ("Do unto others…") or negatively ("Do not do unto others…"), it urges us to remember that our actions ripple outward. What we offer to others shapes the energy we live in.

The Golden Rule echoes something deeper than custom—it aligns with soul-level truth. It whispers: "What you do to another, you do to yourself."

Rooted in Natural Law

Natural Law refers to the inner wisdom that transcends religious doctrine—a knowing accessible through reason, intuition, and conscience. It reminds us that fairness, compassion, and reciprocity aren't cultural constructs. They are spiritual constants.

The Golden Rule springs from that same eternal current. It isn't taught as much as remembered. We feel it in our bones when we act out of kindness—or when we know we've fallen short. To live this way is to live in harmony with Spirit and in alignment with the interconnected web of life.

The Golden Rule Across Traditions

This principle of reciprocity appears across time, land, and lineage. Here are just a few ways the Golden Rule is expressed around the world:

- **Buddhism:** "Treat not others in ways that you yourself would find hurtful." Udana-Varga 5:18
- **Christianity:** "Do unto others as you would have them do unto you." — Matthew 7:12
- **Hinduism:** Impartial everywhere he looks, he sees himself in all beings and all beings in himself. Bhagavad Gita 6:29   One should never do that to another which one regards as injurious to one's own self. This, in brief, is the rule of dharma. Other behavior is due to selfish desires. Brihaspati, Mahabhara`ta (Anusasana Parva, § CXIII, v. 8)
- **Islam:** "None of you truly believes until he wishes for his brother what he wishes for himself." — Hadith, Sahih Muslim
- **Judaism:** "What is hateful to you, do not do to your neighbor." — Talmud, Shabbat 31a
- **Native American:** (Oglala Sioux teaching) "Only act so that the consequences of your actions will be good for the 7th generation."   "All things are our relatives; what we do to everything, we do to ourselves. All is really One" Black Elk
- **Quaker:** "Let your life speak." (A principle that calls for integrity, empathy, and honoring the Light within all people.)
- **Taoism:** "Regard your neighbor's gain as your own gain, and your neighbor's loss as your own loss." — Lao Tzu, T'ai Shang Kan Ying P'ien
- **Wicca:** "An it harm none, do what ye will." — The Wiccan Rede It essentially means that if an action does not cause harm to oneself or others, it is permissible to do it.

Each of these teachings reflects a shared spiritual understanding: how we treat others is a reflection of our relationship to the Divine.

Philosophers on the Golden Rule
The Golden Rule isn't just found in religion — it also appears in the writings of philosophers and ethicists across the ages:
- **Confucius:** "Do not impose on others what you do not wish for yourself." — Analects 15:24
- **Dr. Frank Crane:** "The Golden Rule is of no use to you whatever unless you realize that it is your move." — Early 20th-century writer and spiritual essayist
- **Epicurus:** Believed friendship and kindness were central to a joyful life. His ethics centered around mutual care and simplicity.
- **Epictetus:** (Stoicism) "What you would avoid suffering yourself, seek not to impose on others."
- **Immanuel Kant:** Described a related idea as a categorical imperative: "Act only according to that maxim whereby you can, at the same time, will that it should become a universal law."
- **John Stuart Mill:** His utilitarian ethics urged people to act in ways that produced the greatest good for the greatest number.
- **Plato:** In The Republic, justice is defined as harmony — each person fulfilling their role with integrity. Though not a direct quote, Plato's moral philosophy supports ethical reciprocity and the soul's alignment with the good.

Even Spirit Shows Up in Pop Culture
Sometimes Spirit delivers timeless wisdom through the most unexpected messengers. In **Bill & Ted's Excellent Adventure,** we hear a version of the Golden Rule that's as joyful as it is true: "Be excellent to each other." Simple. Clear. And deeply needed in this world.

Whether from ancient texts or time-traveling teenagers, the message is the same: your choices matter. Your actions ripple outward. Your integrity becomes your offering to the collective spirit.

A Living Practice
The Golden Rule is not about being perfect. It's about being present. It asks us to walk with kindness, speak with intention, and remember that every interaction is an opportunity to align with love. But like all spiritual teachings, it requires discernment.

While the Golden Rule offers a powerful moral compass, it's not one-size-fits-all. What feels kind or thoughtful to you may not feel the same to someone else. For instance, you might enjoy a playful prank — but someone else could experience it as hurtful or disrespectful. That's why empathy matters just as much as intention.

This is where the deeper invitation lies: Not just "treat others as you want to be treated," but "treat others as they would want to be treated." To do that, we must listen, observe, and honor difference. That's the real work — and the real wisdom — behind the Rule. By living this principle with care and compassion, we bring Natural Law into motion — and invite healing into the world.

There is Work Outside of Circle:

Your spirituality is yours. How closely you feel to the Divine/Spirit/God is completely dependent upon your connection. Feeling disconnected? Try one of these methods:
- Meditate daily, focusing on connecting with your higher self and spirit guides.
- Engage in a spiritual practice that resonates with you (e.g., prayer, meditation, nature walks, journaling, or reading sacred scripts are some ways).
- Share your reflections on spirituality and mediumship with a trusted friend.
- Join a church or organization of like-minded people.

Awareness Check: Spirituality & Mediumship

My experience with patience in spiritual growth is often:

a) Feeling restless but trying to stay present
b) Learning to trust timing beyond my control
c) Finding quiet moments where insight arises
d) Struggling to stay open during uncertainty

During moments of waiting or uncertainty, I usually:

a) Try to control the outcome
b) Seek comfort through meditation or prayer
c) Notice what lessons are beneath the surface
d) Feel disconnected from Spirit's flow

How often do I reflect on how natural laws (like cycles or rhythms) show up in my life?

a) Regularly – I see patterns everywhere
b) Occasionally – I notice some connections
c) Rarely – I don't think about it much
d) Not yet – I'm just beginning to explore this

When I honor my personal spiritual pace, I feel:

a) More peace and self-compassion
b) Less pressure to "do it right" or quickly
c) A stronger connection to Spirit's timing
d) I'm still learning to accept my own pace

Group Discussion Questions

- What do you know of Natural Law?
- How has your spirituality changed over the years?
- Can you share a moment when trusting your intuition led you to unexpected guidance or growth?
- In what ways do you honor your unique timing while supporting others on their journeys?
- How do you recognize when you might be pushing too hard versus allowing Spirit to guide you naturally?

Group Exercise – Intuitive Storytelling

- Divide participants into small groups or do as an entire group.
- In groups of 4-5, participants create an intuitive story together. Each person contributes a part of the story based on their intuitive impressions, building on the previous person's contribution.
- One person starts by sharing an intuitive impression or a few sentences of a story.
- Each participant adds to the story based on their intuition, continuing until everyone has contributed.
- After completing the story, the group reflects on the process and the intuitive insights shared.
  - Did anyone anticipate what the next part of the story was going to come from someone? How would this be different from getting a message from Spirit?
  - Could you use this skill to help you ask better questions of Spirit?

Additional Self-Exploration

If this topic feels overwhelming, take a breath—you're not falling behind. Growth can stir up more questions than answers, and that's part of the process. This is an excellent time to revisit earlier topics or exercises with fresh eyes. Each return is a deeper invitation inward, guided by your lived experience. Trust that you're right where you need to be.

How do you live the Golden Rule?

_____
_____
_____
_____
_____
_____
_____
_____
_____
_____
_____

The Golden Rule—and Its Siblings

There are different ways to think about how we treat others, often described as a set of "rules":

- Iron Rule—"Do unto others before they do unto you."
  - A rule of power and self-protection.
- Silver Rule—"Do not do to others what you don't want done to you."
  - Avoid harm, but not necessarily act with kindness.
- Golden Rule—"Do unto others as you would have them do unto you."
  - Treat others as you'd wish to be treated.
- Platinum Rule—"Do unto others as they would want to be treated."
  - Consider the other person's needs and preferences.
- Titanium Rule—"Do unto others with awareness of their trauma and healing journey."
  - An empathetic, trauma-informed approach.

Each "rule" reflects a deeper level of awareness and spiritual responsibility.
Moving from Iron to Titanium invites us to greater compassion and understanding.

Weekly Journal Prompt

This week take time and write each day and answer this question:
How can you remind yourself about not comparing your progress with that of others?

Monday

Tuesday

Wednesday

Thursday

Friday

Saturday

Sunday

Lesson 7 Quiz Answers 1. T 2. F 3. F 4. D 5. B 6. T 7. B 8. T 9. D 10. T

**Reflect on how your understanding of this week's topic has grown.
Consider any personal experiences or new realizations.
Write about what surprised you, challenged you,
or what you feel most drawn to explore further.**

Lesson 8 Quiz

These quizzes are your guide to help you understand what you know and do not know about the topic. This is meant to be helpful in group discussion in your circle work.

1. **True/False**: Tarot cards can be used for both divination and personal reflection.

2. **Which of the following is NOT a typical use for a pendulum?**
    a) Finding lost objects
    b) Communicating with spirit guides
    c) Determining the future
    d) Healing energy fields

3. **True/False**: Divining rods are primarily used for locating water sources.

4. **Which astrological element represents stability and practicality?**
    a) Fire
    b) Earth
    c) Air
    d) Water

5. **True/False**: Numerology is the study of numbers and their influence on human life.

6. **Which color is commonly associated with the heart chakra?**
    a) Red
    b) Blue
    c) Green
    d) Yellow

7. **True/False**: Crystals can be used to amplify energy during meditation.

8. **What is the primary purpose of reading auras?**
    a) Predicting the future
    b) Healing physical ailments
    c) Understanding emotional and spiritual state
    d) Communicating with spirits

9. **True/False**: Each zodiac sign is associated with specific personality traits and tendencies.

10. **Which tool is often used to enhance psychic abilities and intuition?**
    a) Tarot cards
    b) Divining rods
    c) Astrology charts
    d) Pendulums

Notes

Affirmation

I am intuitive, wise, and connected to my inner guidance.

Lesson 8
Your Mediumship Tool Chest
Overview

This week, we explore tools that can enhance your mediumship and spiritual practices. Each tool offers unique properties, helping you connect with Spirit, gain insights, and strengthen your intuitive abilities. Understanding their uses can deepen your practice and expand your awareness. It's equally important to recognize when and how to use these tools. Some mediums believe messages should come solely from Spirit, without relying on external aids. However, for those still learning, tools can be valuable in building confidence and refining your connection. This is a topic worth discussing in your circle, as every medium's journey is unique.

Animal Totems

Animal totems are spiritual guides that appear in the form of animals, offering wisdom, protection, and insight. Each animal carries symbolic meanings and lessons that reflect qualities we can embody or areas we need to pay attention to. Connecting with animal totems helps us deepen our relationship with nature and Spirit, guiding us on our spiritual journey.

Astrology

Astrology is an ancient practice that examines the movements and positions of celestial bodies to gain insight into human affairs and natural rhythms. Your natal chart—based on the time, date, and place of birth—reveals personality traits, life patterns, and spiritual lessons. Astrology helps you understand your gifts, challenges, and purpose, offering a deeper awareness of yourself and your connection to the universe.

Auras

Auras are subtle energy fields surrounding all living beings, reflecting our physical, emotional, mental, and spiritual states. Often seen as color and light, auras shift based on our well-being and energy. Learning to sense or interpret auras can enhance empathy, intuition, and energetic awareness—offering insight into ourselves and those around us.

Chakras

Chakras are energy centers in the body that influence different aspects of life—from physical health to emotional balance and spiritual connection. There are seven main chakras, each linked to specific qualities like safety, creativity, love, or intuition. When balanced, chakras allow energy to flow freely; when blocked, they signal where healing is needed. Working with chakras helps restore alignment and support spiritual harmony.

Dowsing Rods

Dowsing rods—often shaped like an "L"—are tools used to detect subtle energies, water sources, or spiritual presence. Traditionally used for finding underground springs, many now use them to sense energetic fields, ley lines, or Spirit communication. The rods respond to energy shifts in your environment or within a question, helping you tune into unseen information with clarity and intention.

Numerology

Numerology is the mystical study of numbers and their energetic influence. By examining numbers in your name and birthdate, numerology reveals personality traits, challenges, and soul lessons. Each number carries a vibration that can help guide decisions, affirm your life path, and deepen your spiritual understanding. (See page 76.)

Object Reading

In some spiritualist traditions, object reading uses symbolic items—like ribbons, bones, dice, or flowers—as tools during a reading. Each object carries its own energy and meaning, offering insights based on its color, texture, or cultural symbolism. Readers intuitively interpret these objects to deliver personalized messages from Spirit that resonate with the seeker's path.
This practice differs from psychometry, which involves tuning into the energy held by a physical object connected to a person or event. Object reading is active and symbolic, while psychometry is receptive and energetic.

Palm Reading

Palmistry is the art of reading the lines, shapes, and features of the hand to explore personality, emotional patterns, and soul purpose. Your hands tell a story—each line (like the heart line or life line) offers insight into how you feel, relate, and live. The hand's texture, flexibility, and mounts provide even more spiritual symbolism, making palmistry both a personal and intuitive practice.

Pendulums

Pendulums are simple tools used to access spiritual guidance through yes/no questions or energetic sensing. Held steady, a pendulum's movement reflects subconscious knowing or subtle energy shifts. With intention and practice, pendulums can confirm intuition, assist in decision-making, and help detect energetic imbalances.

Runes

Runes are ancient alphabetic symbols that carry spiritual meaning and wisdom. Used for both writing and divination in Nordic traditions, each rune represents a concept like journey, protection, or transformation. When drawn in readings, runes offer guidance, reflection, and connection to natural forces and ancestral energy.

What is Scrying?

Scrying is the practice of gazing into a reflective surface—like a crystal ball, mirror, water, or fire—to receive images, symbols, or insights. It's a meditative, intuitive process that helps you access inner wisdom and spiritual guidance.

Tarot/Oracle Cards

These visual tools support intuitive and spiritual insight. Tarot follows a structured system rich with archetypes and symbolism, while oracle cards vary in theme and imagery. Both invite Spirit to speak through the cards, offering clarity, reflection, and direction on your path. Whether pulled daily or during ritual, cards deepen your relationship with your inner knowing.

Tea Reading

Also known as tasseography, tea reading is the practice of interpreting the shapes and patterns left by tea leaves—or coffee grounds—in a cup. This gentle form of divination taps into symbolism and intuition, offering messages through images that arise naturally. Tea reading encourages you to slow down, observe, and open to subtle guidance from Spirit and your subconscious mind.

Not every spiritual tool will resonate with everyone—and that's not only normal, it's necessary. Each person's path is unique, shaped by their experiences, beliefs, and where they are in their journey. Your connection to a tool depends on what feels authentic and supportive to you in this moment. There is no room for judgment here—neither from others nor from yourself. Tools aren't better or worse; they simply serve different purposes and energies. It's perfectly okay if your preferences shift over time or if a tool you once avoided becomes meaningful later on. The important thing is to honor your own pace, listen deeply to your intuition, and follow what feels right for your growth. Trust that your inner guidance will lead you to the tools and practices that best support your spiritual path. Your inner guidance is your most reliable compass.

NSAC Note

NSAC standards do not condone these tools for the platform.

NSAC does teach as an exploration of things, but the Church does not allow tools from the platform. Just like they do not reference guides, angels or past lives in greetings given from the platform.

For more information please refer to the NSAC Platform Decorum Book.

Your Spiritual Network

No spiritual journey happens in isolation. Your spiritual network is the circle of people, communities, and resources that support your growth, learning, and healing. This may include mentors, fellow seekers, teachers, development circles, books, workshops, or online groups. Building and nurturing your spiritual network provides encouragement, accountability, and shared wisdom. It offers safe space to explore, ask questions, and deepen your connection to Spirit.

To cultivate your network, seek out groups and individuals who resonate with your values and aspirations. Attend workshops or circles that inspire you, and don't hesitate to reach out for guidance or support when you need it. Remember, quality matters more than quantity—choose connections that uplift and honor your path.

Maintaining your network means showing up with openness and authenticity, sharing your journey, and being willing to both give and receive support. Your spiritual network is a living web, evolving as you grow. Trust it to nurture your highest self and help you navigate the twists and turns of your path.

That said, it's important to remember that not everyone in spiritual circles is working from the highest and best intentions. Trust your intuition and set clear boundaries when choosing who to include in your network. Healthy connections honor respect, authenticity, and mutual growth. If you sense energy that feels draining, manipulative, or out of alignment, it's okay—and necessary—to step back. Protecting your energy is a vital part of your spiritual practice and essential for maintaining clarity on your path.

An Invitation to Connect

Your journey matters, and you don't have to walk it alone. If this lesson sparked questions, reflections, or a desire to go deeper, I warmly invite you to connect with me. Whether you're seeking guidance, exploring your spiritual path, or looking to join a community that honors Spirit, I'm here to walk beside you.

You can find more resources, upcoming events, and ways to work with me at:

www.TalkWithColleen.com

I believe in creating safe, grounded spaces where your gifts are honored and your growth is supported.

Let's stay connected—Spirit often brings the right people together at just the right time.

Awareness Check: Spiritual Tool Chest

When I notice others progressing faster than I feel I am, I tend to:

a) Remind myself that my path is unfolding in its own time
b) Feel inspired but sometimes a little discouraged
c) Compare myself and wonder if I'm missing something
d) Pull back and question my abilities

When I try a new spiritual tool, I usually:

a) Dive in with excitement and curiosity
b) Feel a little hesitant but give it a try
c) Need time to warm up before I trust it
d) Avoid it unless I feel a strong pull

I choose spiritual tools or practices based on:

a) What excites or intrigues me
b) What feels gentle and supportive
c) What others have found helpful
d) A mix of intuition and experimentation

I feel most connected to Spirit when:

a) I'm alone in stillness or nature
b) I'm in community or circle with others
c) I'm journaling, creating, or using tools
d) I'm not even trying—Spirit just shows up

Group Discussion Questions

- What has been your experience using Tools?
- In what ways do you feel crystals and auras influence your spiritual and physical well-being?
- How do you discern which tool to use for a specific question or situation?
- What tools do you think would help a person starting out with Mediumship Development.

Group Exercise— Exercise to do as a group

- Set up the room to have multiple stations of two chairs and at each station have a single tool with some instructions and give the pair 5-10 minutes at each play with the tool.
- Suggested tools to have include: Tarot or Oracle cards, Pendulum, Runes, Diving Rods, Book of Astrology, Runes, Ribbons and any other tool you can think of. Have an instruction sheet for someone to read if they are not familiar with the tool.
- Break the participants into A/B, A's will rotate left and B's will rotate right. This way everyone works with other people in the circle and limits the chatter.
- Give 10 minutes with that tool. Rotate the participants through each station as time permits, leaving 15-20 minute at the end to gather everyone together and discuss their experiences with the tools. Some questions to ask:
    - What is your favorite tool? Why?
    - Did you use a tool that you never saw before? Do you think you might use it more?
    - What tool should we explore more of as a group?

Additional Self-Exploration

Tarot Practice

Daily Tarot Practice: Draw a tarot card each morning and journal about its potential message for your day. Reflect on how it applies to your experiences at the end of the day.

Pendulum Practice

Pendulum Meditation: Use a pendulum during your meditation sessions to ask yes/no questions about your current state or decisions you are contemplating. Note any patterns or insights in your journal.

Astrology Practice

Astrology Chart Analysis: Study your natal chart and focus on one aspect (e.g., your moon sign or rising sign). Reflect on how this aspect influences your personality and life experiences. Write about your findings in your journal.

**Describe your favorite tool and why it resonates with you.
What challenges have you faced when learning to use this tool,
and how did you overcome them?**

Weekly Journal Prompt

This week take time and write each day and answer this question:
Spend time with the same tool each day for 10 minutes. What was it like when you started vs. the end of the 7 days you worked with it? Any special insights?.

Monday

Tuesday

Wednesday

Thursday

Friday

Saturday

Sunday

Lesson 8 Quiz Answers 1. T 2. C 3. T 4. B 5. T 6. C 7. T 8. C 9. T 10. A

**Reflect on how your understanding of this week's topic has grown.
Consider any personal experiences or new realizations.
Write about what surprised you, challenged you,
or what you feel most drawn to explore further.**

Lesson 9 Quiz

These quizzes are your guide to help you understand what you know and do not know about the topic. This is meant to be helpful in group discussion in your circle work.

1. **True/False**: Failure is an essential part of the learning process in mediumship.

2. **What is psychometry?**
   a) Reading the energy of objects
   b) Scrying with a crystal ball
   c) Reading tea leaves
   d) None of the above

3. **True/False**: Scrying can be done with tea leaves.

4. **What is one benefit of object readings?**
   a) It helps build confidence
   b) It always gives clear answers
   c) It requires no practice
   d) None of the above

5. **True/False:** Confidence comes from always being right.

6. **Which of the following is not used in object readings?**
   a) Ribbons
   b) Stones
   c) Flowers
   d) all of the above

7. **True/False:** Scrying can be done with a candle flame.

8. **What should you do daily to build confidence in scrying?**
   a) Practice for 10 minutes
   b) Avoid practicing
   c) Only read about it
   d) Wait for group sessions

9. **True/False:** Providing supportive feedback helps build confidence.

10. **Which method is used for reading symbols or images seen in reflective surfaces?**
    a) Psychometry
    b) Object reading
    c) Scrying
    d) None of the above

Notes

Affirmation

"I am confident in my abilities and trust the process of learning."

Lesson 9
Building Confidence
Overview

This week is about strengthening your trust in Spirit—and in yourself. Confidence doesn't come from getting everything right. It grows from experience, exploration, and your willingness to keep showing up. The tools we'll explore—psychometry, object readings, and scrying—are not about performance; they're about connection. Each one offers a different doorway into the unseen, helping you notice what you feel, sense, and receive.

You might not feel confident right away, and that's okay. The point isn't to master the tool overnight, but to learn how Spirit communicates with you through it. Maybe you'll feel drawn to one method and unsure about another. That's part of the journey. Let curiosity lead. Let go of judgment. Trust what comes—and trust yourself enough to keep going. This is a space to practice, to play, and to grow.

Building Confidence

Confidence doesn't arrive all at once—it grows through showing up, trying, and allowing yourself to learn along the way. In spiritual development, especially mediumship, it's easy to doubt yourself when things don't come easily or clearly. But every impression, every attempt, even every silence, is part of the process. Confidence builds when you stop chasing perfection and start trusting your own rhythm. Give yourself permission to get it "wrong." Spirit isn't grading you—they're growing with you. Stay curious, stay compassionate, and keep practicing. The more you trust, the more Spirit can flow through you.

Confidence Boosters

- **Regular Practice and Reflection** - Dedicate time daily to practice your mediumship skills and keep a journal of your experiences. Consistent practice and reflecting on your progress build familiarity and confidence.
- **Positive Self-Talk and Visualization** - Replace negative thoughts with positive affirmations and visualize yourself successfully performing tasks. Positive self-talk and visualization reinforce your confidence.
- **Step Out of Your Comfort Zone** - Challenge yourself to try new things and set achievable goals. Each step outside your comfort zone and every small achievement build momentum and confidence.
- **Celebrate Small Wins** – Keep track of the moments that went well, no matter how small. Celebrating progress—rather than perfection—nurtures long-term confidence.

Discussion and Reflection

This lesson offers rich opportunities for sharing and learning together. Building confidence is a personal journey, but it can also be strengthened by hearing others' experiences, challenges, and breakthroughs. Take time to discuss your thoughts on psychometry, object readings, and scrying with your circle or study group.

What feelings come up when trying these tools? How do you navigate doubt or uncertainty? How does trusting Spirit show up differently for each of you? These conversations can deepen your understanding and remind you that you're not alone on this path.

Group Discussion Questions

- How does understanding that failure is part of the learning process change your approach to mediumship?
- How does EGO play into your confidence, or lack thereof, with your mediumship?
- Why do you think we call it a Mediumship practice?
- How do you recognize when you're listening to Spirit versus your own inner critic?
- Why do we feel perfection is the only way?
- What strategies help you stay grounded and centered when doubt arises during a reading?
- Can you share a moment when trusting your intuition led to a breakthrough or confirmation?
- How do you balance patience with the desire to progress quickly in your development?
- In what ways can community or a spiritual network support your confidence?
- How do you handle situations where the messages you receive feel unclear or incomplete?
- What role does compassion—for yourself and others—play in building your mediumship confidence?

Friendly Reminder:

Setbacks are a normal part of your spiritual journey.

Each challenge is an opportunity to learn, grow, and deepen your connection.

Be gentle with yourself and keep moving forward—progress isn't always linear.

Awareness Check: Building Confidence

When I encounter a challenge in my mediumship practice, I usually:

a) See it as a learning opportunity
b) Feel frustrated but keep going
c) Doubt my abilities for a while
d) Consider giving up

How often do I trust my first impression/gut feeling during a reading?

a) Almost always
b) Often, but I double-check
c) Sometimes, but I second-guess myself
d) Rarely or never

How do I approach new spiritual tools?

a) With excitement and openness
b) With cautious curiosity
c) With skepticism or hesitation
d) I tend to avoid trying new tools

Which statement best reflects my current relationship with Spirit in my mediumship?

a) I feel connected and trust the process
b) I'm learning to trust but have doubts
c) I doubt Spirit's communication through me.
d) I feel disconnected and question my abilities

Group Exercise — Psychometry

One of the easiest ways to support learning is for the facilitator to bring a selection of personal items for circle members to read, offering feedback on the impressions received from each object.

If not, an excellent exercise will need you to have an identical set of envelopes.

- Have each person put their drivers license, or similar card from their wallet in an envelope, including the facilitator. Have each person seal the envelope.
- Put the pile of envelopes in the center, Conduct a 5-10 minute focus meditation for the group.
- After the meditation, give each person one envelope, and have them write on it any impressions.
- Give everyone 2 minutes per envelope until everyone has written an impression.
- At this point, the envelope that each person has they should write their name on the bottom of it.
- Give every member an opportunity to keep their envelope or swap with someone else.
- Once you have done that, go around the circle and have the person read their envelope's impressions and then reveal the card inside.
- Did it match the name on the outside? If not, give the id back to that person. Have the person who's id it was let the group of anything that made sense to them. Once they have shared it is their turn to reveal the envelope they had.
- Another way to do this exercise is with postcards in envelopes or have participants bring a 4x6 photo to share. Be creative, have fun. It is part of the learning process.

Additional Self-Exploration

__Daily Scrying Practice__

Dedicate 10 minutes each day to practice scrying using your preferred method. Record your experiences in your journal.

__Object Reading Practice:__

Select different objects around your home or in nature. Spend a few minutes with each object, noting any impressions or feelings that arise. Record these in your journal.

> **How do you feel after practicing psychometry and object readings?**
> **What new insights did you gain about your abilities?**

Weekly Journal Prompt

This week take time and write each day and answer this question:
What steps can you take to continue building your confidence in mediumship?

Monday

Tuesday

Wednesday

Thursday

Friday

Saturday

Sunday

Lesson 9 Quiz Answers: 1. T 2. a) 3. T 4. a) 5. F 6. d) 7. T 8. a) 9. T 10. c)

**Reflect on how your understanding of this week's topic has grown.
Consider any personal experiences or new realizations.
Write about what surprised you, challenged you,
or what you feel most drawn to explore further.**

Lesson 10 Quiz

These quizzes are your guide to help you understand what you know and do not know about the topic. This is meant to be helpful in group discussion in your circle work.

1. **The primary responsibility of a medium is to:**
    a) Solve clients' problems
    b) Provide spiritual guidance
    c) Offer medical advice
    d) Predict the future

2. **True/False:** It is ethical to make decisions for clients during a reading.

3. **A key component of ethical mediumship is:**
    a) Charging high fees
    b) Maintaining confidentiality
    c) Guaranteeing outcomes
    d) Predicting specific events

4. **True/False:** A medium should refer clients to professional help if it appears that they need it.

5. **Ethical boundaries in mediumship include:**
    a) Offering legal advice
    b) Giving specific medical diagnoses
    c) Providing compassionate support within limits
    d) All of the above

6. **True/False:** It is acceptable to share personal client information with others.

7. **An example of a professional resource for a client in crisis and has mentioned they are suisidal:**
    a) A friend's advice
    b) A general self-help book
    c) National Suicide Prevention Lifeline (988)
    d) An online forum

8. **True/False:** Mediums should always act in the best interest of their clients.

9. **Responsibility in mediumship includes:**
    a) Predicting the lottery numbers
    b) Providing legal services
    c) Offering spiritual insights while respecting boundaries
    d) Diagnosing mental health issues

10. **True/False:** Maintaining professional boundaries is not important in mediumship.

Notes

Affirmation

"I practice my mediumship with integrity, compassion, and a deep sense of responsibility."

Lesson 10
Responsibilities and Ethics
Overview

Mediumship is a sacred responsibility, one that requires more than just skill—it calls for integrity, discernment, and compassion. This lesson invites you to reflect on the ethical foundation of your practice and the importance of boundaries, both with Spirit and with the living.

You are a guide, not a fixer. Your role is to share what comes through with honesty and care—without overstepping into areas better handled by trained professionals. You are not a doctor, therapist, lawyer, accountant, auto mechanic, or appraiser. It's not only wise to avoid those topics, it's your ethical duty to gently remind your sitter to seek professional advice when needed.

Some regions may also have legal requirements, like stating that "Readings are for entertainment purposes only." Even when it feels unnecessary, including that disclaimer is a form of protection—for both you and your sitter. It keeps expectations clear and prevents confusion.

Ethical mediumship means showing up with humility, compassion, and a willingness to put the sitter's well-being first. You don't need all the answers. You just need to serve with honesty and heart.

Boundaries With Spirit

One of the greatest gifts I received on this journey was understanding that I am not the only way a message can reach someone. Spirit will always find another way.

For a long time, I believed I had to respond to every nudge, every message, every pull from Spirit. I thought it was my responsibility to say yes, always. But that belief left me overwhelmed and energetically drained.

Setting boundaries with Spirit doesn't block the connection—it strengthens it. It honors the relationship. Spirit respects clarity. When you set an intention for when and how you're available, Spirit responds accordingly.

You have permission to rest. You have permission to say, "Not right now." And you have the right to create a practice that sustains you, not one that consumes you.

Boundaries aren't barriers. They're the framework that allows you to serve with love, confidence, and longevity.

Creating a Contract with Spirit

A contract with Spirit establishes a respectful, structured relationship with the spiritual realm. This intentional agreement outlines your expectations, boundaries, and ethical guidelines for spiritual work. By clearly defining what you will and won't engage with, you create a safe, controlled environment aligned with your highest good.

Somewhere along the way, one of my teachers introduced me to the concept of creating a contract with Spirit. I don't recall exactly who, but it was a powerful game changer for me — and that's why I share it here.

Knowing I could set clear boundaries and say no when working with Spirit was huge for me. Before this, I believed I had to respond to everything and deliver every message. Realizing there is always a way — and that I am not the only channel — freed me in many ways.

Regularly revisiting and updating your contract ensures it evolves with your spiritual growth, fostering mutual respect and understanding with Spirit.

Example Contract With Spirit

When creating a contract with Spirit, I prefer to write it in my own handwriting, sign, and date it. I keep the contract in my journal as a reminder of my intentions. When I revise it, I write "CANCELLED" across the old version, tear it up and burn it — a personal ritual that helps me release the past and embrace the updated agreement.

You might choose a different method; the key is to make it meaningful for you. Don't hesitate to update your contract regularly as your spiritual practice evolves. Start by listing everything — what you will and won't work with, your working hours, and any specific boundaries or expectations. Over time, you can refine it further.

This contract is between Colleen Irwin and Spirit, in any form. I rescind all prior contracts with Spirit. I will only work for the highest and best for all involved, this includes me. To that effect, I do not deal with Spirits that wish to make amends for any form of abuse. It is assumed that I am closed unless I invoke Spirit and once I close it is not a time for negotiation. Please lovingly find another way, there is always another way. When I am driving, in the bathroom or my bed, these areas are off limits. I authorize my Gate Keeper to assist me in giving the information I need to give uplifting messages and to keep Spirit away when I am not working. These rules are in effect now until I change them.

Build Your Own Contract With Spirit

Use this form to answer questions that will help you write your own contract with Spirit. Know that as you grow in both confidence and ability this may change for you.

What days of the week and hours are you willing to work with Spirit?	
When and where do you want Spirit to never bother you?	
What exactly are your intentions?	
Where do you want them to stand?	
How do you want them to communicate with you?	
What kind of messages do you not want to work with?	
Do you want Spirit to work in a specific way?	
How will you let Spirit know you are open/closed?	
Other rules/guidelines you want to set with Spirit.	

Personal Ethical Code

I am sharing my personal Code of Ethics here. Write your own that will help you with boundaries with sitters and your personal contract with Spirit. Many organizations have their own Code of Ethics that you may be required to adhere to when working in their environment.

Professional Standards

- I treat this as a profession, as such I come dressed appropriately and come prepared to do the work, rested and not distracted.
- I build up the profession of Mediumship by providing education through published works as well as teaching classes and participation in development circles. Work with others to correct any misrepresentations and enhance the public's understanding of Lightworkers.
- As this is a practice, I regularly attend continuing education and further the profession by learning new aspects of serving Spirit.
- I volunteer time assisting those in need and if I am unable to assist them, direct them to resources for the correct assistance. Volunteering includes serving at local churches and organizations for their fundraisers. This includes the public demonstrations at Lily Dale that I do.
- I respect fellow Lightworkers, by never publicly demeaning them. Disputes are handled privately and if need be there is always a way to handle a situation professionally.

Public Interaction

- Accept that the person sitting has Free Will and that I will not pass judgement on their decisions.
- Messages given are only for the highest and best of the sitter, I will not give messages of hate or deal with angry souls.
- I do not discriminate based on race, age, gender, sexual orientation or national origin. I believe love is love and will protect it.
- For anyone under the age of 18 sitting for a reading, I first request the parent or guardian to sit with the child.
- I reserve the right to not read for someone who is obviously high or drunk and I will not do readings under the influence.
- I am not a doctor, lawyer, accountant, auto mechanic or appraiser. If you desire this type of information, I will recommend seeking proper professional assistance.
- I cannot guarantee that the reader will hear from whom they wish to hear or that it is what they want to hear. I can guarantee that it is what Spirit believes they need to hear at the time.
- I will not touch someone without first obtaining positive consent.
- I maintain confidentiality to all clients and the contents of readings. If I write about our encounter, details will be changed and/or omitted to protect you.

Build your own code of ethics. Between the Code of Ethics and your Contract With Spirit, you will have confidence that Spirit will be working with you for the highest and best for all.

Church Based Mediumship Organizations

- National Spiritualist Association of Churches (NSAC) – www.nsac.org
- Spiritualists' National Union (SNU) – www.snu.org.uk

Awareness Check: Responsibilities & Ethics

When I receive a message that touches on health or medical issues, I usually:

a) Share it gently, then suggest they follow up with a healthcare provider
b) Feel unsure whether or not to say anything
c) Try to interpret it myself
d) Avoid sharing it altogether

If a sitter asks for legal or financial advice, I tend to:

a) Remind them I'm not qualified and suggest seeking a professional
b) Feel tempted to answer
c) Say something vague and hope it helps
d) Redirect them to a different question

When I feel pressure to "perform" during a reading, I:

a) Remind myself I'm just the messenger, not the source
b) Try harder and hope something comes through
c) Get flustered and lose confidence
d) Push through, even if I'm not sure what I'm getting

I believe a responsible medium should:

a) Know when to say "I don't know"
b) Always have an answer
c) Try to give people what they want to hear
d) Avoid difficult conversations

Group Discussion Questions

- Reflect on a time when you set a boundary. How did it feel when it was crossed?
- How do you define ethical mediumship?
- What values guide your mediumship practice?
- What does "working for the highest and best" mean to you personally?
- Describe a time you referred a client to a professional. How did you handle it?
- What strategies ensure you maintain ethical standards?
- How do you handle client requests beyond your scope as a medium?
- Have you ever witnessed questionable ethical behavior in a spiritual setting? How did you respond? How might you respond differently now?
- Share an experience where you made an ethical decision during a reading. What was the outcome?
- How do you address situations involving unethical practices by others?

Group Exercise — Ethics Practice

Here are two exercises (one centered around the entire circle and one where participants can practice different situations):

- **Ethical Scenario Analysis:** Discuss various ethical dilemmas a medium might face and brainstorm appropriate responses. Use group discussion questions.
- **Role-Playing:** Pair up and role-play different client scenarios to practice setting boundaries and referring clients to appropriate professionals.

National Resources for Professional Help

It is a good idea to have a list of resources with you when you are doing private readings. It is important to refer someone in crisis to professionals. It is important to build your own list of resources for someone. You won't need it often, but when you do it is an awesome thing to be able to give them the help they need with confidence. Below is a limited list of national resources:

Suicide Prevention:
- National Suicide Prevention Lifeline: 1-800-273-8255 (Available 24/7) or 988
- Crisis Text Line: Text HOME to 741741 (Available 24/7)

Domestic Abuse:
- National Domestic Violence Hotline: 1-800-799-7233 (SAFE) (Available 24/7)

Grief Counseling:
- GriefShare: 1-800-395-5755,
- National Hospice and Palliative Care Organization: 1-800-658-8898

Mental Health Support:
- National Alliance on Mental Illness (NAMI): 1-800-950-6264 (NAMI)
- SAMHSA's National Helpline: 1-800-662-4357 (HELP) (Available 24/7)

Substance Abuse:
- Substance Abuse and Mental Health Services Administration (SAMHSA): 1-800-662-4357 (HELP) (Available 24/7)

How do you balance the need for compassion with the necessity of maintaining professional boundaries?

Weekly Journal Prompt

This week take time and write each day and answer this question:
Each day this week, reflect on where you say something that is not kind. Reflect on how you can improve going forward. Do you need to apologize for the lack of kindness?

Monday

Tuesday

Wednesday

Thursday

Friday

Saturday

Sunday

Lesson 10 Quiz Answers 1. B 2. F 3. B 4. T 5. D 6. F 7. C 8. T 9. C 10. F

**Reflect on how your understanding of this week's topic has grown.
Consider any personal experiences or new realizations.
Write about what surprised you, challenged you,
or what you feel most drawn to explore further.**

Lesson 11 Quiz

These quizzes are your guide to help you understand what you know and do not know about the topic. This is meant to be helpful in group discussion in your circle work.

1. **Telepathy involves:**
    a) Predicting future events
    b) Communicating through the mind without the five senses
    c) Viewing distant locations without being physically present
    d) Reading body language

2. **True/False:** Precognition can occur through dreams and flashes of insight.

3. **Remote Viewing is the practice of:**
    a) Sending thoughts to another person
    b) Predicting events based on current information
    c) Gathering information about a distant or unseen target
    d) Healing through touch

4. **True/False:** Telepathy can enhance empathy and understanding between individuals.

5. **The skill of perceiving a specific location:**
    a) Telepathy
    b) Remote Viewing
    c) Precognition
    d) Clairvoyance

6. **True/False:** Remote Viewing requires physical presence at the target location.

7. **Which ability is most likely to be experienced during sleep?**
    a) Telepathy
    b) Precognition
    c) Remote Viewing
    d) Clairaudience

8. **True/False:** Developing these abilities requires trust in one's intuition and patience.

9. **The practice of perceiving details about distant locations is:**
    a) Clairvoyance
    b) Telepathy
    c) Precognition
    d) Remote Viewing

10. **True/False:** Precognitive insights are always accurate and clear.

Notes

Affirmation

"I trust my inner wisdom and the guidance of the universe."

Lesson 11

Precognition, Remote Viewing & Telepathy

Overview

This lesson explores intuitive abilities that stretch our perception—telepathy, precognition, and remote viewing—and how to discern their presence in your spiritual development. These were mentioned in Lesson 6 on page 75, but they are powerful tools you will use.

Telepathy is the ability to send or receive thoughts, emotions, or impressions without speaking. It's often subtle—like knowing what someone is about to say, sensing their emotions before they express them, or receiving a phrase that wasn't your own thought. In mediumship, telepathy may be how Spirit "drops in" a message or image.

Precognition is the intuitive awareness of events before they happen. This might come through a vivid dream, a flash of insight, or simply a sense of "knowing." It's not about predicting everything—it's about noticing when those nudges align with truth, often confirmed in hindsight.

Remote Viewing involves perceiving people, places, or situations beyond your immediate surroundings. You're not physically present, but you may receive images, details, or sensations connected to a location or object. Think of it as tuning into a frequency that exists outside of time and space.

We'll also explore the difference between subjective and objective experiences in mediumship, helping you identify how Spirit communicates with you. Are you seeing images in your mind's eye or sensing something outside of yourself?

You may also wonder: "Is this Spirit… or just my imagination?" That's natural. We'll lean into that question and show how both imagination and intuition can work together.

Lastly, we'll talk about healthy skepticism—not as a block to Spirit, but as a helpful tool. Discernment keeps us grounded, encourages integrity, and helps you become a confident, trustworthy practitioner.

This lesson invites curiosity, practice, and reflection—offering space to try, question, and grow. These abilities aren't reserved for a gifted few—they're skills you can strengthen over time. Many development circles revisit these practices regularly, helping participants deepen their trust, sharpen their awareness, and build confidence through shared experience and support.

Skepticism in Mediumship

Skepticism plays a vital role in mediumship, ensuring authenticity and credibility. Mediumship often involves intangible abilities like telepathy, precognition, and remote viewing, which naturally invite doubt. However, skepticism encourages mediums to rigorously test their experiences, fostering truth and integrity in their work.

By embracing healthy skepticism, mediums can refine their abilities, distinguish genuine insights from imagination, and build trust with those they seek to help. It becomes a tool for growth, pushing mediums to stay grounded and committed to delivering meaningful, verifiable messages.

Subjective vs. Objective Mediumship

Understanding the difference between subjective and objective experiences is essential for interpreting spiritual communication effectively.

Objective mediumship involves perceiving spirit messages through physical senses. For example, with objective clairvoyance, you might see a spirit person as if they were physically present. Similarly, objective clairaudience involves hearing spirit voices outside your body, as though in the physical world. These experiences feel external and tangible.

Subjective mediumship, on the other hand, is internal. Subjective clairvoyance involves seeing images or symbols in your mind's eye, while subjective clairaudience is hearing spirit within your thoughts. These impressions are personal and often require interpretation, as they can be influenced by your beliefs and emotions.

Discernment strengthens trust in spirit communication. By distinguishing your thoughts from true spirit messages, you deepen your connection. Both forms of mediumship are valid—trust your journey as each step brings greater clarity.

Imagination or Spirit?

Ask the spirit world, "Show me something randomly." This takes patience, but wait until an image pops into your mind without thinking about it first. If you haven't previously thought about the image, you can count on it as being something from the spirit world. Got it?

Now let the image fade away and completely clear your mind. Next, ask the spirit world, "Show me something that has significant meaning for me." Wait. Don't force it! Soon, an image will pop into your mind. Whether it makes sense or not, you'll realize it's a picture you would have never previously thought of. The more you practice, the more precise the images will become.

Awareness Check:

Skepticism in mediumship helps me:

a) Reject messages that don't fit my beliefs
b) Stay grounded and seek truth
c) Avoid trusting Spirit altogether
d) Perform readings faster

When an image or message pops into my mind without prior thought, it is likely:

a) Pure imagination
b) A message from Spirit
c) Something I want to believe
d) Random noise

Distinguishing between imagination and Spirit requires:

a) Forcing clear images or answers
b) Practicing patience and noticing what comes naturally
c) Ignoring subtle impressions
d) Asking others to interpret for me

Telepathy involves:

a) Hearing Spirit voices externally
b) Receiving thoughts or feelings from another mind without words
c) Predicting future events
d) Seeing images in a crystal ball

Group Discussion Questions

- How accurate were any, if any so far, precognitive insights you may have had, and what factors might influence their accuracy?
- What was your experience with remote viewing, and how did it feel different from other forms of perception?
- What was your experience with remote viewing, if you've tried it?
- How do you tell the difference between messages from Spirit and your imagination?
- What role does skepticism play in your spiritual practice?
- Can you share a time when skepticism helped you gain clarity or avoid confusion?
- How do you experience subjective vs. objective perceptions during readings?
- How do you stay patient when waiting for clear intuitive messages?
- In what ways has practicing discernment deepened your trust in your abilities?

Group Exercise – Telepathy with Deck of Cards

- Break everyone up into pairs, have them sit back to back.
- Designate one to be the sender, the other the receiver. Using a standard deck of cards give the senders each a card.
- Ask the senders to send for 1 minute, ask the receiver to state what they feel was sent their way.
- Swap roles and repeat the exercise.. Then change partners and give everyone the opportunity to work with every other member of the circle.
- Regroup in the circle and discuss the experience of the exercise.

Additional Self-Exploration

Remote Viewing with Deck of Cards

- Take a standard deck of cards and shuffle them.
- Have a small notepad to denote your responses before revealing the card. You will need three columns, Criteria, Guess, & Correct Answer.
- Criteria could be: Court Cards, Number Cards, black/red, Clubs, Hearts, Spades or Diamonds, a specific card (king) or the entire deck
- Shuffle the deck between attempts
- Silence your mind and ask Spirit to look at the card and tell you what will be turned over.

This is a great exercise in working with your guides. Any time you are feeling stuck, it is also helpful in building your connection with Spirit.

This could also be used as a telepathy exercise with a partner.

Describe a time when you had a strong intuitive feeling about something. What was the outcome?

Weekly Journal Prompt

This week take time and write each day and answer this question:

Each night this week, keep track of your dreams and what you remember first thing in the morning. Write about your impressions and feelings about these dreams.

See Lesson 6 for more about dreams.

Monday

Tuesday

Wednesday

Thursday

Friday

Saturday

Sunday

Lesson 11 Quiz Answers: 1. B 2. T 3. C 4. T 5. C 6. F 7. B 8. T 9. D 10. F

**Reflect on how your understanding of this week's topic has grown.
Consider any personal experiences or new realizations.
Write about what surprised you, challenged you,
or what you feel most drawn to explore further.**

Lesson 12 Quiz

These quizzes are your guide to help you understand what you know and do not know about the topic. This is meant to be helpful in group discussion in your circle work.

1. **True/False:** Self-care is only about physical activities.

2. **What is an essential component of a self-care routine?**
    a) Exercise
    b) Sleep
    c) Nutrition
    d) All of the above

3. **True/False**: Meditation can be a form of self-care.

4. **What should you include in a self-care plan?**
    a) Activities you enjoy
    b) Activities you feel obligated to do
    c) Activities others recommend
    d) None of the above

5. **True/False:** Self-care practices can enhance your mediumship abilities.

6. **How often should you engage in self-care activities?**
    a) Daily
    b) Weekly
    c) Monthly
    d) Occasionally

7. **True/False:** Self-care is a one-size-fits-all approach.

8. **Which of the following is a sign you need more self-care?**
    a) Feeling overwhelmed
    b) Feeling balanced
    c) Feeling rested
    d) None of the above

9. **True/False:** Keeping a self-care journal can help you track your progress.

10. **Which chakra is associated with grounding and security?**
    a) Root
    b) Sacral
    c) Solar Plexus
    d) Heart

Notes

Affirmation

"I trust my intuition to guide my self-care."

Week 12
Self-Care in Mediumship
Overview

Self-care is not a luxury—it is an essential part of a healthy and sustainable mediumship practice. A well-rested, grounded person will always navigate spiritual work with more clarity and ease than someone depleted or overwhelmed. Some traditions suggest specific diets or routines, and many mediums choose to abstain from alcohol or recreational drugs. Others find their own rhythms through lived experience.

The truth is, there's no one-size-fits-all approach. What works beautifully for one medium may not work at all for another. Your job is to stay curious, stay compassionate, and keep tuning in to your body and spirit. Self-care isn't just bubble baths or meditation—it's boundaries, rest, nourishment, movement, stillness, and grace.

When we are tired or pushing past our limits, we can't be fully present in service to Spirit or to others. Learning to trust your body's signals is a skill, and like all skills, it gets better with practice. Your energy is your most important resource. Protect it.

Personal Reflection

I've had to step away from my work with Spirit more than once—especially during periods of physical healing, like surgery. Each time, I honored my need to rest, recover, and rebuild. I discovered I couldn't be on pain medication, do the physical work of healing, and also open myself to Spirit in a healthy way. It wasn't just about balance—it was about boundaries. I realized that I mattered.

During my first surgery, I feared I'd lose my connection. I thought time away would mean losing progress. But when I returned, it was like I never left—actually, it felt easier. My link to Spirit had grown stronger during that time because I honored myself. Since then, I've learned the value of shutting down when needed. It gives me space to come back clearer, calmer, and even more connected.

We are first and foremost human beings. Life will bring moments where mediumship needs to pause—and that's not failure, that's wisdom.

A Gentle Reminder

Every medium's path is different. Some will fast before sitting. Others won't. Some may take months off, others won't feel the need. Resist the urge to compare or judge. What someone else needs is not a reflection on what you need.

We grow by honoring both our own process and the sacredness of another's. Self-care is a personal and spiritual responsibility, not a performance. Choose what nurtures you. Respect others as they do the same.

Ways to Take Care of Yourself

There is a lot of talk that we need to take care of ourselves, but you may be wondering how to do so. Here

- **Grounding and Centering:** Techniques like walking barefoot or using grounding crystals stabilize energy. Helps prevent energy drain and keeps you balanced.
- **Regular Meditation:** Daily meditation quiets the mind and strengthens your connection to spirit. Reduces stress and enhances intuition.
- **Healthy Diet:** Eating nutritious, whole foods supports physical and mental health. Improves energy levels and overall well-being.
- **Physical Exercise:** Regular activity like yoga or walking keeps the body fit. Reduces stress and boosts energy.
- **Energy Clearing:** Practices like smudging or salt baths clear negative energy. Maintains a positive and clear energy field.
- **Boundaries and Downtime:** Setting limits on mediumship work ensures regular breaks. Prevents burnout and maintains balance.
- **Journaling:** Writing thoughts and experiences provides an emotional outlet. Helps process feelings and track growth.
- **Connecting with Nature:** Spending time outdoors helps recharge and ground your energy. Reduces stress and provides grounding energy.
- **Regular Sleep:** Prioritizing good sleep hygiene ensures you are well-rested. Improves mood, physical health, and mediumship abilities.
- **Community and Support:** Connecting with other mediums provides encouragement and learning. Offers support and fosters growth.

Closing Thought

Care for yourself like you care for your practice—tenderly, honestly, and without judgment. Spirit always honors your humanity.

Cord Cutting

Cord cutting is a powerful self-care practice for mediums to release negative or draining energetic connections. These can form between individuals, places, or situations, often resulting in feelings of fatigue, emotional heaviness, or being overwhelmed. By consciously severing these connections, mediums can reclaim their energy and maintain their spiritual health. The process involves visualizing or meditating on the cutting of these cords, often using tools like crystals or affirmations to enhance the ritual. Regular cord cutting helps mediums stay clear, focused, and balanced, ensuring they are not weighed down by unwanted energies and can continue their work with clarity and strength.

Awareness Check: Self-Care

How often do you intentionally make time for rest and recovery?

a) Daily
b) A few times a week
c) Only when I feel burned out
d) Rarely — I tend to push through

What's your biggest challenge with self-care right now?

a) Time and scheduling
b) Guilt or permission to rest
c) Not knowing what I really need
d) Consistency and follow-through

Which of these best describes your self-care approach?

a) Intentional and consistent
b) I try, but it's not regular
c) It happens only in emergencies
d) I struggle to make space for it

What is your relationship with setting personal boundaries for your energy?

a) Strong — I set and maintain them well
b) Developing — I'm learning to honor them
c) Weak — I have a hard time saying no
d) I haven't thought much about it yet

Group Discussion Questions

- How do you balance your mediumship practice with your personal life?
- What self-care practices have you found most effective?
- How does self-care impact your connection with spirit?
- What has taking a break from Spirit work taught you — if you've done it?
- How do you recognize when your energy is depleted, and what do you do next?
- Do you feel judged by others about your self-care? Do you care what they think?
- Why do we have such a difficult time taking care of our own needs?
- Do you ever say yes when you want to say no? How does that feel?

Group Exercise — Spirit Connection Circle

- Sit in a circle and do a 10-15 minute meditation with your participants. In this meditation, encourage participants to connect with one of their guides and ask them to join them for the rest of the circle. Ask their guide to give a piece of advice for the circle as a whole.
- Share each guide's advice for the group. Then, go around the circle and take turns sharing messages prompted by the facilitator (Color, animal, word, name) — let everyone try and have each recipient give quick feedback. The idea is the first thing that pops into the participants head. There is no right/wrong choice.
- Each member will focus on connecting and delivering messages to others in the circle, enhancing their connection.
- After the exercise, take time to discuss how that felt.

Additional Self-Exploration

Take a Break

This week take a break from specific exercises on your own. Take a walk, enjoy a hobby, go to a movie, do something that brings you joy.

> **Write the story of how you discovered Mediumship was something you wanted to explore.**

Weekly Journal Prompt

This week take time and write each day and answer this question:

This week take time each day and write down things you see, feel, hear, taste or smell that you believe are signs from Spirit. Remember to thank Spirit every time you get these signs.

Monday

Tuesday

Wednesday

Thursday

Friday

Saturday

Sunday

Lesson 12 Quiz Answers: 1. F 2. D 3. T 4. A 5. T 6. A 7. F 8. A 9. T 10. A

**As you complete the 12 lessons, reflect on your initial intentions and goals.
How have you grown, and what new insights have you gained?
Set a few intentions for the coming season based on what feels ready to deepen or evolve.**

Full Circle Self-Test

1. **True/False:** Grounding can help improve focus and concentration.
2. **Meditation primarily helps in:**
    a) Distracting the mind
    b) Enhancing spiritual connection
    c) Physical exercise
    d) Shopping

3. _____ is the sending and receiving thoughts without the five senses.

4. **True/False:** Mindfulness means being aware of the present moment without judgment.
5. **Which of the following is a common protection technique?**
    a) Shielding
    b) Overeating
    c) Watching TV
    d) Ignoring emotions

6. Regular _____ practices are essential for maintaining energy balance in mediumship.

7. **True/False:** Clairsentience is the ability to taste messages from spirits.

8. **Which clair ability involves receiving messages through sounds or voices?**
    a) Clairaudience
    b) Clairvoyance
    c) Clairsentience
    d) Claircognizance

9. _____ involves seeing visual messages from the spiritual realm.

10. **True/False:** Building trust with Spirit can enhance the accuracy of mediumship readings.
11. **Spiritual growth can be achieved through:**
    a) Meditation and mindfulness
    b) Ignoring spiritual practices
    c) Multitasking
    d) Overworking

12. **Which ability allows a medium to know information about future events?**
    a) Telepathy
    b) Precognition
    c) Remote viewing
    d) Clairaudience
    e)

13. _____ can help provide insights about future events.

14. **True/False**: Spirituality is solely based on religious practices.

15. **Which tool is used for divination through symbols carved on stones or wood?**
    a) Astrology Charts
    b) Pendulums
    c) Tarot cards
    d) Runes

16. _____ is the ability to perceive details about a distant or unseen target.

17. **True/False:** Mediumship can facilitate emotional healing for clients.

18. **Which practice helps in sending healing energy to others?**
    a) Remote healing
    b) Clairvoyance
    c) Listening to loud music
    d) Eating junk food

19. Ethical mediumship involves acting with honesty and _____.

20. **True/False:** Ethics in mediumship involve respecting client confidentiality.

21. **Which practice can help improve grounding?**
    a) Arguing
    b) Watching TV
    c) Overeating
    d) Walking barefoot on grass

22. **Building trust with Spirit involves:**
    a) Consistent practice and patience
    b) Ignoring spiritual messages
    c) Overthinking every detail
    d) Distrusting intuitive feelings

23. **True/False**: Telepathy can be practiced with both people and animals.

24. _____ is the ability to feel the emotions or physical sensations of spirits.

25. **Which practice helps in maintaining energy balance?**
    a) Regular self-care
    b) Ignoring personal needs
    c) Overworking
    d) Multitasking

26. **True/False**: Using tools like pendulums and Tarot cards can improve intuitive skills.

27. Which spiritual tool is based on interpreting the positions and movements of celestial bodies?
   a) Runes
   b) Tarot cards
   c) Astrology
   d) Pendulums

28. Regular _____ can enhance intuitive abilities and promote spiritual growth.

29. True/False: Regular self-care practices are essential for maintaining energy balance in mediumship.

30. Which practice involves using crystals for healing and protection?
   a) Crystal healing
   b) Numerology
   c) Astrology
   d) Runes

31. Which of the following is a benefit of regular meditation?
   a) Physical exhaustion
   b) Increased stress
   c) Enhanced intuitive abilities
   d) Constipation

32. _____ fields, also known as auras, surround living beings.

33. True/False: Self-care practices can prevent burnout.

34. Which of the following is a form of mediumship that involves communication with animals?
   a) Telepathy
   b) Precognition
   c) Remote viewing
   d) Clairaudience

35. Which clair ability involves feeling the emotions or physical sensations of spirits?
   a) Clairsentience
   b) Clairvoyance
   c) Clairaudience
   d) Claircognizance

36. Which of the following practices is essential for ethical mediumship?
   a) Respecting client boundaries
   b) Making exaggerated claims
   c) Ignoring feedback
   d) Overpromising results

37. _____ is the ability to hear messages from the spiritual realm.

38. **Which practice can enhance intuitive skills?**
    a) Regular use of divination tools
    b) Ignoring intuitive feelings
    c) Overthinking decisions
    d) Avoiding spiritual practices

39. **True/False:** Building trust with Spirit requires consistent practice and patience.

40. **Which clair ability is also known as clear seeing?**
    a) Clairsentience
    b) Clairvoyance
    c) Clairaudience
    d) Claircognizance

41. _____ is a form of mediumship that involves communication with animals.

42. **True/False:** Ethics in mediumship involves ignoring client boundaries.

43. **Which practice helps in centering energy?**
    a) Deep breathing
    b) Listening to loud music
    c) Arguing
    d) Overeating

44. Using tools like Tarot cards and pendulums can _____ intuitive skills.

45. **True/False:** Clairvoyance involves clear seeing.

46. **Which of the following is a common benefit of grounding techniques?**
    a) Improved focus and concentration
    b) Increased stress
    c) Physical exhaustion
    d) Disconnection from reality

47. Building trust with Spirit requires consistent _____ and patience.

48. **Which practice can enhance spiritual growth?**
    a) Binge Eating
    b) Ignoring emotions
    c) Meditation/Prayer
    d) Watching TV

49. **True/False:** Mediumship only benefits the medium.

50. _____ is the practice of being aware of the present moment without judgment.

**Imagine you are preparing to start a circle or teach others.
What key insights would you share? How would you encourage a beginner?
This exercise will help you solidify your growth and prepare for the next steps in your journey.**

_____

Answer Key Full Circle Self-Test:
1. T, 2. b, 3. Telepathy, 4. T, 5. a, 6. self-care, 7. F, 8. a, 9. Clairvoyance, 10. T, 11. a, 12. b, 13. Precognition, 14. F, 15. d, 16. Remote viewing, 17. T, 18. a, 19. integrity, 20. T, 21. d, 22. a, 23. T, 24. Clairsentience, 25. a, 26. T, 27. c, 28. meditation, 29. T, 30. a, 31. c, 32. Energy, 33. T, 34. a, 35. a, 36. a, 37. Clairaudience, 38. a, 39. T, 40. b, 41. Telepathy, 42. F, 43. a, 44. enhance, 45. T, 46. a, 47. practice, 48. c, 49. F, 50. Mindfulness

Full Circle: Weaving It All Together

You've reached the final chapter in this Development Circle journey—a sacred milestone. Twelve lessons. Countless moments of connection, discovery, and growth.

Maybe you feel confident now—more in tune with Spirit, clearer in your mediumship skills, and ready to step forward with faith and trust. You've opened doors to new ways of seeing and hearing, and you carry that knowing with you.

Or maybe you feel like Charlie Brown on Halloween—holding your rock, wondering if this is all there is. That's okay. Spirit's language isn't always loud or clear at first. Sometimes, what feels like a "rock" is the seed of something much greater.

Whether you feel triumphant or uncertain, remember this: mediumship and spiritual development is a journey of unfolding. It's not about instant mastery, but about showing up, listening, and growing over time.

Spiritual development isn't a straight line. It's a spiral—each turn bringing you back to familiar ground, but with fresh insight, deeper trust, and more courage. Now is the time to pause and reflect. Look back on your journals, your exercises, your moments of clarity and confusion. See the transformation, both subtle and profound.

Ask yourself:
- What calls me forward—what is ready to deepen next?
- Where did I experience resistance, and what might that resistance be asking me to explore?
- In what moments did I trust Spirit—or myself—even just a little more than before?
- How has my definition of "success" in mediumship shifted over the past twelve weeks?
- Have I been gentle with myself during moments of doubt or frustration?
- What moments (even small ones) made me feel like I belonged in this work?
- How can I assist others on their spiritual path?
- Who in this circle assisted or inspired me the most, and how did they impact my growth?
- What do I need to feel more supported on this path?
- Which skills feel steady, and where do I still hold uncertainty?
- How would I like to show up next time—with more curiosity, trust, or intention?
- Where have I stretched beyond what I thought possible?
- What would I love to give myself more permission to experience next time around?
- When did Spirit's presence feel closest—or most elusive?
- What might I be more open to in a future circle experience?

No matter where you are on this path, you are seen, supported, and honored. This isn't an ending—it's a spiral, circling back with new wisdom and a fuller heart. You're not starting over; you're beginning again, this time with experience by your side.

Guidance for the Facilitator

This final gathering is intentionally unstructured. Come with no agenda—just presence. Let the space be guided by the questions, reflections, and needs of the group. Participants may wish to revisit certain lessons, clarify concepts, or simply share what's shifted for them.

Trust the process. If conversation flows for the entire session, allow it. Spirit often speaks most clearly in those moments of open-hearted sharing. Sometimes, it's the way someone says something that opens the door for another's breakthrough.

After this session, invite a pause—a week or two to rest, reflect, and reset. When you're ready to begin again, consider setting the guidebook aside. Invite participants to journal freely, noticing what arises without prompting.

With my long-standing groups, we often take a natural breather after Week 6 to review and tie what we know together. It isn't a rule, just a rhythm. Sometimes that pause brings the deepest growth of all.

When you begin the next cycle, remember that spiritual development is a spiral—not a straight line. You might choose a different order for the lessons or spend more time exploring a particular topic that calls to the group. This is your journey—fluid, evolving, and deeply personal.

And remember—there are no fixed rules. Even the most experienced participant will discover something new in the foundations. This path doesn't end. It expands. Each cycle brings you back around, but with new insight, deeper wisdom, and fresh light to guide your way.

This is not the end of the journey. It's simply a moment to catch your breath before continuing. Because in spiritual development, no one is ever truly "done." We're all still learning. Still deepening. Still becoming.

Facilitator Affirmation/Prayer

May I hold this sacred spiral with humility and grace.
May I welcome each return as an invitation to deeper growth.
May I honor every step—seen and unseen—as part of the unfolding path.
And may I create space for Spirit's wisdom to flow freely through each circle,
each heart, each moment.

Meditations

Meditation is an essential part of Mediumship Development. It helps participants ground and center themselves, become present in the moment, and prepare their minds and bodies for the deeper spiritual work ahead. Through meditation, we can set the intention for our exercises, clear our energy, and connect more deeply with Spirit.

By guiding your participants through focused, calming meditations, you help them create a strong foundation for their practice. Trust your intuition as a facilitator, and remember that flexibility is key—adapt the meditations as needed to best serve your circle.

It's important to recognize that not everyone finds meditation easy. Some participants may struggle to quiet their minds or sit still for long periods. For this reason, I recommend keeping meditations short and focused, particularly at the beginning. This approach allows everyone to benefit from the practice without feeling overwhelmed.

Guiding a Meditation: There are many ways to guide students through a meditation. Rember, the structure provided here is not a rigid standard.

- Keeping students in the circle for the mediation is best. Ask them to find a comfortable position and ensure that their cell phones and other distractions are silenced.
- I prefer to guide meditations without music, as this allows participants to focus on my voice without the distraction of background sounds. However, this is not a strict rule—there are times when music can enhance the meditation experience, especially if it's used to create a specific mood or atmosphere.
- As the facilitator, you are free to adapt the meditations to suit the circle. Whether you choose to use music, silence, or a combination of both, the key is to create a space where participants feel relaxed, focused, and ready to engage with Spirit.
- I often begin each meditation with a relaxation exercise. This helps to calm the participants, release physical tension, and ground their energy. By using the same relaxation technique consistently, participants become familiar with the process, which can make the transition into deeper meditation smoother and more effective.
- Here's a basic relaxation script that I use regularly (next page). It's flexible enough to be shortened or lengthened depending on the needs of the session.

Adapting Meditations

As you continue to facilitate meditations, you may find that certain themes or visualizations resonate more strongly with your group. Don't hesitate to adapt the basic script to suit different intentions that align with the topic at hand, such as connecting with guides, enhancing intuitive abilities, or focusing on healing. The foundation provided here is just the beginning on which to build, creating meditations that align with your group's specific needs and goals.

Relaxation Script Opening

1. Sit comfortably and just breathe.
2. Close your eyes and take a deep, cleansing breath in through your nose. Hold it for 3, 2, 1, and now breathe out every bit of tension through your mouth. As you do, feel the tension release from your feet and toes. Wiggle your toes to ensure they are relaxed. Imagine roots growing from the bottom of your feet, reaching deep into the earth, anchoring you to its center. You are now grounded and centered.
3. Take another deep breath in through your nose. Hold it for 3, 2, 1, and exhale all the tension from your ankles, calves, and knees. Feel the tension leave your lower legs, and as it does, you begin to feel lighter, more at ease.
4. Breathe in deeply again. Hold it for 3, 2, 1, and release the tension from your thighs and hips. As the tension melts away, feel yourself sinking comfortably into your chair, fully supported and relaxed.
5. Take another deep breath in. Hold it for 3, 2, 1, and as you exhale, let go of any tightness in your stomach and diaphragm. You're now feeling calm, centered, and peaceful.
6. Take another deep, cleansing breath. Hold it for 3, 2, 1, and as you exhale, feel the tension release from your chest and shoulders. Your shoulders relax, and the tension slides down your arms, through your hands, and drips out of your fingertips.
7. Finally, breathe in deeply one more time. Hold it for 3, 2, 1, and as you breathe out, feel the tension drain from your neck and head, all the way to your crown.
8. As the last of the tension leaves your body, imagine a bright white light descending from above, filling you with love, understanding, and readiness to work with Spirit."

Now begin any visualization or meditation you wish to insert.
[These begin on the next page.]

Relaxation Script Closing

1. Please thank your Spirit guides for joining us for this meditation.
2. I am going to count down to ten, slowly bring back your attention back to this space, open your eyes and be ready to discuss.
3. 10, 9, 8, 7, 6, 5, 4, 3, 2, 1   Welcome back.

After Meditation Discussion

After meditation, go around the circle and discuss what was seen/felt during the meditation. Encourage everyone to share the oddest details or messages that they received during the meditation. The hardest part of this is people's willingness to share. I often share from the least experienced to the most. This eliminates the *"well what I felt/saw/heard is dumb compared to..."*

Tree of Wisdom Meditation

1. Today, we are going to visit the Tree of Wisdom, a special place where Spirit communicates with us through the energy of an ancient, powerful tree.
2. Imagine yourself walking along a peaceful path in a forest. The air is cool, and the ground beneath your feet feels soft with moss. As you walk, you notice a large, majestic tree ahead of you, its roots deep and its branches reaching high into the sky.
3. This is the Tree of Wisdom, where you can sit and connect with Spirit. As you approach the tree, notice the texture of its bark, the sound of the leaves rustling in the breeze, and the feeling of ancient energy emanating from it.
4. Find a comfortable spot at the base of the tree, or perhaps climb into one of its sturdy branches. Sit quietly and ask Spirit to share any wisdom or messages that you need to hear today.
    Give participants 3-5 minutes with Spirit.
5. As the meditation comes to a close, thank the Tree of Wisdom for its guidance. Know that you can return here anytime for insight and support.

Ocean of Insight Meditation

1. Today, we will journey to the Ocean of Insight, where Spirit shares messages through the rhythm and flow of the waves.
2. Picture yourself standing on a warm, sandy beach. The sky is a soft shade of pink as the sun sets, casting a golden glow on the gentle waves lapping at the shore.
3. Walk slowly toward the water, feeling the cool sand between your toes. As you reach its edge, notice how the waves seem to be speaking to you, whispering messages from Spirit.
4. Allow yourself to wade into the water, feeling the coolness against your skin. As you float gently on the surface, ask Spirit for the guidance or insight you need. The answers may come through the movement of the water, the sound of the waves, or the colors of the sunset.
    Give participants 3-5 minutes with Spirit.
5. As the meditation ends, let the ocean carry away any worries or doubts, leaving you feeling refreshed, clear, and connected to Spirit.

Library of Knowledge Meditation

1. Today, we will visit the Library of Knowledge, where Spirit reveals messages through books, reference materials and ancient scrolls.
2. Visualize walking down a quiet hallway lined with tall wooden doors. One door calls to you—it leads to the Library of Knowledge. Each door has a different bit of wisdom for you. No choice is incorrect.
3. Push it open and step inside. The vast room is filled with rows of shelves holding ancient books and scrolls, and the air carries the scent of wisdom.
4. Walk through the library until a book or scroll feels meant for you. Pull it from the shelf and find a quiet place to sit. Open it and ask Spirit to reveal the message or knowledge you need. Observe the words, images, or feelings that arise.
    Allow participants 3-5 minutes to connect with Spirit.
5. When ready, gently close the book, thanking Spirit and the Library of Knowledge for the insights received.

Safe Place Meditation

1. Today, I want you to go to your safe space that you talk to Spirit and your guides.
2. For me it is a field of Dandelions on a warm sunny day and the sky is crystal blue with a few white puffy clouds. There is a willow tree on the edge of the field, and I climb the tree and sit and communicate with Spirit there. Picture your safe and peaceful space for yourself.
3. Ask your guides for any guidance they have for you or messages for someone in the circle.
   Give participants 3-5 minutes with their guides.
4. Remember when I bring you back please thank Spirit for this time and tell them that you will be back soon to visit again.

Clothing Meditation

1. We are going to use the image of a Suit of Clothes to assist you with the message you are going to share in circle. Ask Spirit to share what members of the circle need to know right now. In doing so, Spirit is going to put clothing on you to help express this wisdom to the circle.
2. Ask Spirit to put clothing on you. As you see this outfit in the full-length mirror in front of you notice:
   3. How elaborate does it look? What is the condition of the outfit?
   4. How did they feel? Were they loose or tight fitting? Comfortable or stiff?
   5. What textures did you sense? What colors did Spirit choose for you?
   6. What accessories did your outfit have?
3. Ask Spirt for a message that you will bring back to circle.
   Give participants 3-5 minutes with their guides.

See how the description of the outfit helps convey the message.

Variations and Alternatives to Phrases

We're all different, so there's more than one way to say things. You might find a phrase that fits you better—and that's perfectly okay. Here are some commonly used phrases in meditation.

Variations to the "Deep cleansing breath in…"at the start of a meditation:
- Breathe in positivity, exhale negativity
- Inhale confidence, exhale doubt
- Draw in peace and calm, and release stress and frustration
- Breathe in light and clarity, exhale tension and worry.
- Inhale love and gratitude, exhale fear and resistance.
- Draw in strength and balance, release what no longer serves you.
- Breathe in renewal and energy, exhale exhaustion and overwhelm.

Alternative Prompts:
- If at any time you are distracted, come back to your breathing.
- If your mind wanders, gently bring your awareness back to your breath.
- Let your breath be your anchor, guiding you back to the present moment.
- Simply notice your breath—no need to control it, just observe.
- If distractions arise, acknowledge them and return to your natural rhythm of breathing.
- Your breath is always here for you—return to it whenever you need.

Meet Your Guides Meditation

1. This meditation will help you connect with your spirit guides.
2. Find a comfortable seated position with your feet firmly on the ground, and gently close your eyes. Take a moment to settle into your space, adjusting your posture until you feel truly comfortable.
3. Begin by taking a deep breath in through your nose, filling your lungs with fresh, revitalizing air. As you exhale through your mouth, release any tension in your body, letting go of stress and worries. Repeat this deep breathing a few more times, with each breath in, inviting positivity and with each breath out, releasing negativity.
4. Imagine a beautiful radiant light above your head, like a glowing sun. This light represents pure source of energy. With each inhale, draw this radiant light down into your body through the top of your head, your crown chakra. Feel it flow down through your head, your neck, your shoulders, and into your heart center. As it enters your heart, let it expand, filling you with warmth, love, and positive energy.
5. As you exhale, imagine any negative emotions, fears, or worries being released from your body and dissolving into the universe, where they will be transformed into positivity. With each breath, feel yourself becoming more and more grounded.
6. I want you to visualize roots growing from the soles of your feet, extending deep into the earth. These roots reach down through the soil, past rocks, and deep into the Earth's core. You are now firmly connected to the loving energy of Mother Earth. Feel her strength and support beneath you.
7. Now, let's ensure our protection for this spiritual journey. Imagine a radiant cloak surrounding your entire being. This cloak is made of the strongest spiritual material, providing you with unwavering protection at all times. You are safe and secure within this protective cloak. It is always with you when you communicate at the spiritual level.
8. Picture yourself in a serene forest clearing, surrounded by tall trees, vibrant flowers, and gentle animals. The warm sun above you radiates a comforting glow, bathing you in its golden light. You are sitting on a wooden bench, feeling completely safe and at ease.
9. One of these gentle animals may come and sit beside you, smile and acknowledge their presence. Notice the sky is a brilliant blue with a few white clouds that create a familiar image. Note what that is.
10. In the distance, you notice a majestic mountain. Look closely, and you'll see a narrow, winding path leading down from the mountain. Two radiant white lights gracefully descend this path, moving slowly towards the forest where you sit. As they approach, you see a gate, and the lights pause outside it, waiting for your permission to enter this sacred space.
11. I want you to focus on this gate, what it looks like and who may be there meeting these guides waiting for your approval for them to come into your scared space. Note the size of the gate, is it made of stone, wood, or metal. What color is the gate. Notice the path that leads from the gate to your bench. What is it made of? Are there plants that you recognize. Is there anything decorative along the path?
12. Now turn your attention back to the two lights near the gate. Notice if you feel a presence—perhaps an angel, an ancestor, or simply a strong, loyal energy. You may recognize this presence as your gatekeeper or protector. Even if you don't see them clearly, you might sense trust, familiarity, or calm. They affirm that the Guides stepping forward are for your highest and best, and they honor your boundaries with Spirit.

13. You give them a nod of approval, allowing them to enter the forest. These lights draw closer to you, and in their presence, you feel a profound sense of peace and tranquility. You recognize that you are in the presence of higher spirits, your spirit guides.
14. Extend a welcoming gesture to the first light source, and kindly ask, "What is your name?" Pay close attention to any sensations, emotions, symbols, music, colors or aromas that accompany their response.
15. These will serve as your unique connection with this guide. Inquire about their purpose – whether they are here to teach, guide, inspire creativity, or offer specific assistance. You may also ask, "Can I trust you?" Trust is something your guide expects to earn over time.
16. Feel free to ask your spirit guide any questions that weigh on your mind. Seek guidance for turning points in your life, career choices, breaking out of a rut, or solving dilemmas.
17. Listen closely for their responses and thank your spirit guide for their wisdom. Observe as this guide gracefully steps back, allowing the second spirit guide to step forward.
18. Now, ask the second guide for their name, noting any unique symbols or sensations. Instead of asking a question for specific guidance from this guide just ask, "What guidance do you have for me today?" Listen attentively to their responses, as they offer insights to guide you on your path. Trust anything that comes into your thoughts. You are not imagining these thought, they are purposely coming to you in this moment. Remember that this is what they believe is important and for your highest and best. At all times you have free will and can do with this information what you wish.
19. After receiving guidance, express your gratitude, and observe as both light sources retire. They retreat through the gate and ascend the mountain path, gradually fading into the distance. You find yourself back on the bench, basking in the warmth of the sun, surrounded by comfort, peace, and serenity.
20. Now thank your gatekeeper for their assistance in this meditation. Ask them to show you a sign in the coming week that they are not too far away from you. Pay attention to any sensations you may have in your body, smells that may uniquely identify them to you. Be open to their unique way to express themselves to you.
21. Now, slowly bring your awareness back to your physical body. Begin to gently wiggle your fingers and toes, returning to the present moment. When you're ready, open your eyes, fully aware of your surroundings.
22. Carry the feeling of well-being and the wisdom gained from your spirit guides you throughout the rest of your day. Whenever you need guidance, remember this connection and trust that your spirit guides are always there to support and assist you on your journey.
23. I am now going to count back from 10, when I reach zero, bring yourself back to this place and time and jot down any thing you wish to remember from this meditation. 10,9, 8….

Note:

You may wish to discuss this meditation afterwards and not have any planned exercises.

It generally creates a lot of questions and discussion is helpful if there are a lot of new people to the circle. Items mentioned in the Meditation to help discussion:

- Cloak of protection
- Wooden bench
- Gentle Animal sitting next to you
- White clouds creating an image
- Majestic Mountain
- Description of Gate
- Description of Path
- Guide 1 – Ask for Advice (specific)
- Guide 2 – Open to Advice
- Gatekeeper
- Sign from gatekeeper

Group Based Exercises

Here are group based exercises you can do in circle as your move beyond the initial 13 weeks of this book. Explore other options if these exercises do not work for you. Sometimes there is a time and a place for exercises. What doesn't work this week, may just work next month.

Partner Thought Transmission

Objective: Enhance telepathic communication between individuals.
Instructions:
- Sit quietly with a partner.
- One person thinks of a simple image or word and tries to send it mentally to the other. The receiver writes down or draws what they perceive. Numbers and Letters are a good place to start.
- Compare results and switch roles.

Act It Out: Understanding the Roles of Messages

This exercise illustrates the process and demonstrates how a Gatekeeper organizes Spirit communication to help the Medium deliver clear messages. It also shows the chaos that can arise without boundaries, providing participants with a deeper understanding of these roles.

Objective: To illustrate how a Gatekeeper filters Spirit communication, ensuring clarity for the Medium and Sitter, and to contrast this with the disorganization caused by unfiltered Spirits.

Roles:
- **Sitter:** Receives the message and represents someone learning the process of connecting with Spirit.
- **Medium:** Delivers the message from Spirit to the Sitter. The facilitator can play this role or assign it to a participant.
- **Gatekeeper:** Filters and organizes Spirits, deciding which one communicates with the Medium.
- **Spirit A:** Chosen by the Gatekeeper to communicate. This Spirit whispers the message to the Medium.

Spirits B, C, D, etc.: Represent unorganized Spirits trying to communicate simultaneously until redirected by the Gatekeeper.

Instructions:
1. **Assign Roles:** Assign participants to each role, explaining their purpose briefly.
2. The Medium sits with the Sitter to deliver the message.
3. The Gatekeeper stands nearby, filtering Spirits.
4. Spirits B, C, D, etc., initially try to overwhelm the Medium with chaotic attempts to communicate.

Controlled Communication: The Gatekeeper organizes the Spirits, selecting Spirit A to deliver the message. Spirit A whispers the message to the Medium, who relays it to the Sitter.

Demonstrating Boundaries:
- **Without Boundaries:** Let Spirits B, C, D, etc., bombard the Medium all at once, creating chaos. The Medium acts overwhelmed, showing how confusing and ineffective communication becomes.
- **With Boundaries:** Redirect Spirits through the Gatekeeper. The Gatekeeper selects Spirit A, while the remaining Spirits wait in line. Highlight the difference in clarity and control.

Discuss the Takeaways:
- After the exercise, gather the group for a discussion. Ask the Sitter how it felt to receive the message. Did it make sense? Was it clear?
- Ask the Gatekeeper how they managed the Spirits and whether it was challenging to maintain order.
- Discuss with the Medium how it felt to deliver the message with and without the Gatekeeper's assistance.
- Encourage the participants to share their thoughts and any new insights gained from the exercise.

Purpose:
- **For the Sitter:** To understand how messages are organized and delivered by the Medium, and how the presence of a Gatekeeper can facilitate clearer communication.
- **For the Medium:** To experience the importance of having a Gatekeeper and setting boundaries with Spirits.
- **For the Gatekeeper:** To learn how it is to put the boundaries up and how much easier it is to work with Spirit.
- **For Spirits B, C, D:** To reinforce all of the above and learn patience.

Intuition and Trust Building through Partner Reading

Objective: Build trust in intuition and strengthen connections with Spirit through partner exercises.

Instructions:
- Pair up the participants.
- Each pair sits facing each other and takes a few moments to center themselves with deep breathing.
- One partner closes their eyes and focuses on receiving intuitive messages or symbols for their partner.
- The person with closed eyes shares any images, feelings, or symbols that come to mind without filtering or overthinking.
- The receiving partner provides feedback on how these messages resonate with their current life situation or spiritual journey.
- Switch roles and repeat the process.
- After both partners have shared, switch up partners. Leave enough time to discuss as a group the different symbols and messages received, highlighting the importance of trusting one's intuition.

Where to Find Meditations, Exercises and Journal Prompts

There are endless resources out there—books, websites, and your fellow circle leaders will all have tools to share. What I've included here is just a starting point. Consider it a jump start, not a full resource kit.

As your trust in Spirit deepens and your confidence grows, you'll begin to create your own inspired meditations, exercises, and journal prompts—ones that speak directly to the needs of your circle. And trust me: those will often be the most powerful tools of all.

Symbol and Object Reading

Participants take turns selecting an object and intuitively reading its energy and meaning for the group.

Instructions:
- Gather a variety of objects and symbols (e.g., crystals, coins, small figurines or pull from your toolchest).
- Place the objects in a bag or box.
- Participants take turns drawing an object and sharing any intuitive impressions they receive about it.
- You can ask other members of the circle to share their impressions with the same object.
- The group provides supportive feedback and discusses the impressions

Blind One-on-One Readings

Instructions:
- Group Setup—Divide the circle into Group A and Group B.
- Have Group A sit in chairs facing a wall, arranged in a straight line. Ensure there is enough space between each person to maintain privacy.
- Position each of the Group B standing behind a different member of Group A.
- Instructions for Group B—Tap the left shoulder if you relate to the information being shared. Tap the right shoulder if they cannot relate.
- Time the Exercise - Set a timer for 1 minute per round.
- Group A members will share whatever impressions, messages, or details they receive.
- Group B provide silent feedback using the shoulder taps only—no verbal communication allowed.
- Rotate Roles—Have A's stand and B's sit. Once they are seated, place a different person behind the person sitting.

Additional Variations:
- Do a reading where there will be no feedback until the end, and have the person seated then tell them that someone is behind them, just do not put anyone there.
- Have the person connecting with Spirit focus on a specific topic/feature:
  - Sex of the Spirit, Personality, Career, what the sitter needs to know
  - Spirit's Cause of death, favorite {item/place}
  - Focus on the aura of the person they are reading
- Instruct the people getting the reading to
  - Always say Yes
  - the next time to always say no

Debrief as a Group
- Discuss the experience. Encourage participants to share insights, challenges, or surprises from both roles.
- This exercise helps students practice tuning in without relying on verbal or visual feedback, strengthening their intuitive and psychic abilities.

The Name Game

Instructions:
- This is a good exercise to do with 10 or more people. If you have a smaller number, you can do it with the entire group. You will need to break the circle up into two or more teams (keep to approximately 5 people on a team)
- The premise of this is to run through the alphabet A – Z and name as many names as you can through the group without repeating a name. If a name is repeated, you have to start over with the letter which a name was repeated.
- Each letter of the alphabet the team has to use 5 (feel free to change up the number) times so Adam, Andrew, Andrea, Alan, Alice – then you move onto the next letter until you get to Z. First team wins.
- Letters Q, U, V, X, Y, Z name three.

My home circle does this as an exercise to "warm up" - as a group we keep track of how many names we can come up with in 2 minutes.

Circle of Light

Instructions:
- Form a Circle: Have participants stand or sit in a circle, holding hands if comfortable.
- Breathe Together: Begin with several deep breaths, inhaling and exhaling in unison.
- Visualize Light: Ask everyone to close their eyes and visualize a bright light in the center of the circle.
- Expand the Light: Imagine the light expanding outward, connecting and enveloping everyone in the circle.
- Share the Energy: After a few minutes, invite participants to share how they feel, fostering a sense of connection and unity.

Intuitive Drawing Exercise

Instructions:
- Materials: Blank paper, colored pencils or crayons.
- Sit in a circle and give each participant a sheet of blank paper and colored pencils or crayons.
- Ask everyone to close their eyes and take a few deep breaths to center themselves.
- Guide them to focus on a question or intention related to their mediumship journey.
- With eyes closed or slightly open, allow the participants to draw or doodle whatever comes to their mind, without overthinking.
- After 5-10 minutes, invite everyone to share their drawings and discuss any insights or feelings that arose during the exercise.

Group (also called Shared or Threaded) Readings

Instructions:
- Arrange participants in the circle
    - I like to mix people us by strength so someone stronger sits in between two newer
    - Move family members or close friends apart
- Do a brief meditation to get everyone focused.
- Select a person in the circle and designate them as the sitter. Have everyone else give in turn their impressions of a Spirit with that person. See if you can as a group pull a message together for the sitter.
- After you are done with the first message, get feedback from the sitter. Choose another person and repeat until all members of the circle have had the opportunity to be the sitter.
- Once done, review how that felt to everyone. Here are some questions you may wish to pose to further the discussion or suggest participants journal about:
    - Did you find yourself having more confidence as you heard other's impressions?
    - Did someone else's impression help clarify or expand on what you were sensing?
    - How did you feel about the overlap or differences in impressions?
    - Did you notice a shift in the group's energy as the exercise progressed?
    - How did the collective energy impact your ability to connect?
    - What did you like/dislike about this type of message?
    - Did you have an "aha" moment during this exercise?
    - What surprised you most about what you picked up during this exercise?
    - How did this exercise become easier/harder as you moved through recipients?
    - Did you notice any patterns in the types of messages or information you tend to receive?
    - Did you notice a stronger connection to the recipient after hearing other impressions?
    - How did the group's impressions collectively help the recipient?
    - Did working as part of a group feel different from doing readings alone?
    - How do you feel about the feedback you received from the recipient and the group?
    - What feedback would you give yourself after this exercise?

Color Readings

<u>Setup:</u>

Prepare multiple sets of index cards:
- Set 1: Basic colors written in black ink
- Set 2: Basic colors written in the color (red, orange, green, blue, purple, pink, black).
- Set 3: All cards have the same color (e.g., blue, purple or red).
- Set 4: Basic colors, but the word is written in a different color than what it says.
- Set 5: Advanced and unique colors (e.g., coral, teal, lavender, bronze, maroon).

<u>Instructions:</u>

Partner Work — Divide the group into pairs and have them spread out in the room.
Partners sit face-to-face to create an energetic connection.

Step 1: Basic Colors

Hand each participant an index card from set 1

Each participant focuses on their card's color for one minute in silence.

Their partner then tunes in and shares the color impression they receive.

After feedback, swap roles within the pair.

Step 2: Same Color for Everyone

Hand out index cards from set 2

Follow the same process: focus for one minute, then share impressions.

Rotate partners before moving to the next step. (Tip: This step builds confidence by increasing accuracy rates.)

Step 3: Mismatched Color Cards

Hand out cards from set 3

Participants focus on the written color name, not the ink color.

Partners share impressions, then roles are reversed.

Rotate partners before moving to the next step.

Step 4: Expanded Color Selection

Use cards from set 4 or 5

Follow the same process: focus for one minute, share impressions, and swap roles.

<u>Group Debrief:</u>
- Gather everyone in a circle to discuss their experiences and impressions.
- Suggested questions for discussion:
- What techniques helped you connect with the colors?
- Was it easier to sense common colors or unique ones?
- How did working with mismatched colors affect your focus?
- Did you notice patterns or preferences in how you receive impressions?

Self Exploration Exercises

These exercises can help participants deepen their spirituality and enhance their mediumship practice through personal reflection and connection with the spiritual realm.

Spirit Walk
- Go for a nature walk, focusing on being present and connecting with the natural world around you.
- Pay attention to the sights, sounds, and sensations you experience. As you walk, silently invite any spirit guides or loved ones in spirit to join you.
- After your walk, journal about any insights or feelings that came to you during this time.

Sacred Space Creation
- Dedicate a small area in your home as a sacred space.
- Decorate it with items that hold spiritual significance to you, such as crystals, candles, or spiritual symbols.
- Spend a few minutes each day in this space, meditating or simply sitting quietly, inviting spiritual guidance and connection.

Daily Gratitude Ritual
- Each morning or evening, write down three things you are grateful for.
- Reflect on how these blessings are connected to your spiritual journey and mediumship practice.
- This exercise helps to cultivate a positive mindset and reinforces your connection to a higher power.

Intuitive Art
- Create a piece of art that represents your spiritual journey and mediumship.
- Use any medium you are comfortable with, such as drawing, painting, or collage.
- Allow your intuition to guide you as you create.
- Reflect on the process and the final piece, noting any messages or insights that emerge.

Spirit Letter Writing
- Write a letter to a loved one in spirit or to your spirit guide.
- Express your thoughts, feelings, and any questions you may have.
- After writing the letter, sit quietly and open yourself to any responses or impressions that come to you.
- Journal about the experience and any messages you receive.

Symbol Research
- Choose a symbol that you encounter frequently or feel drawn to.
- Research its historical, cultural, and spiritual meanings.
- Reflect on how these meanings resonate with your personal experiences and spiritual journey.
- Write a short essay or journal entry about your findings and personal reflections.

Symbol Interpretation
- Select a symbol (e.g., a feather, a key, a heart) and meditate on its meaning for you.
- Throughout the week, notice when and where this symbol appears in your life.
- Record these occurrences and your interpretation of their significance in your journal.

More Advanced Solo Practice

<u>Purpose:</u>
Strengthen your connection with the spirit world by practicing intuitive impressions about people close to you.

<u>Steps:</u>
Select a Focus Person—Think of someone you know well and feel a connection with (friend, family member, etc.).

Set Your Intention
Take a few calming breaths to center yourself. Mentally ask the spirit world: "Please show me something significant about [Person's Name]."

Open to Receive
Sit quietly and remain open to any impressions you receive.
Pay attention to images, words, feelings, or sensations.
- You might see a specific object, place, or event.
- You could sense emotions or hear words, phrases, or names.
- You might even feel inspired to focus on a specific time frame (e.g., "last week" or "coming soon").

Interpret the Message
Reflect on what you received and what it might mean.
Example: If you see a car with its hood up, you might sense it relates to car trouble.

Validation
The next time you talk to this person, casually ask them about what you sensed.
For instance: "Have you had car trouble recently?" Take note of their response without overthinking it.

Record Your Results
Write in your journal immediately after the exercise. Include:
- Date: Always note when you did the exercise.
- Person's Name: Who you focused on.
- Impressions: Every detail you received, even if it seems unrelated.
- Validation: Note their response and whether the information made sense.
- Keep track over time—some impressions may not make sense immediately but could align with future events.

<u>Tips for Success:</u>
Be Patient: Don't worry if your impressions feel unclear or unrelated at first. Trust that your skills will improve with practice.
Stay Neutral: Avoid overanalyzing or doubting your initial impressions. Write them down as you receive them.
Practice Regularly: Repetition builds confidence and sharpens your ability to interpret messages.
Celebrate Small Wins: Even a minor hit (like guessing a small detail) is progress!

Journal Prompts

These prompts are to help you continue journaling each week on a different topic. Instead of being told what to write, pick one of these topics and reflect each day on the topic for the week, or decide on a new prompt each day. The important thing is to journal each day. Here are some suggested prompts:

1. Reflect on a time when you felt ungrounded. How did you regain your stability?
2. Describe your current meditation routine. What benefits have you noticed?
3. Reflect on a healing session you conducted. What emotions surfaced for you?
4. Write about a recent intuitive insight. How did it impact your day?
5. Describe a significant sign or symbol you've received recently. What did it mean to you?
6. Describe your experience with a new meditation technique.
7. How do you recharge your energy?
8. Explore how each of your senses contributes to your mediumship. Which one needs more attention?
9. Reflect on your spiritual journey and its impact on your mediumship skills.
10. List the tools you currently use. How does each one support your mediumship?
11. How do you validate the messages you receive?
12. Write about a time when you doubted your abilities and how you overcame it.
13. Identify areas in your practice where you feel less confident. What can you do to improve?
14. Reflect on a situation where you had to make an ethical decision. What did you learn?
15. Describe an instance where you used telepathy or precognition. What was the outcome?
16. Evaluate your current self-care routine. What can you improve or add?
17. What practices help you strengthen your intuition?
18. Reflect on the role of intuition in your daily life.
19. Write about your first experience connecting with a spirit guide.
20. Reflect on the presence of a loved one who has passed.
21. How do you handle conflicting intuitive messages?
22. How do you differentiate between your thoughts and messages from Spirit?
23. How do you develop and trust your psychic senses?
24. Reflect on a situation where you felt guided by Spirit.
25. How do you protect your energy during spiritual work?
26. What boundaries do you find most challenging to uphold?
27. Write about a time someone crossed one of your boundaries. How would you hand that differently now?
28. Write about what feels unfair in the world? What can you do to help correct it?
29. What music makes you feel calm?
30. Who is your biggest influence in your life lately?

Additional Topics to Discuss

Now that you've completed this guidebook, you may want to revisit topics or explore new ones. Use this list as inspiration for deeper reflection — on your own or with your circle.

If you're a self-guided group, consider assigning topics and sharing what you discover. As your group settles, you may find less need for discussion and more space for practice and new exercises.

Spiritual development moves in a spiral. Each time you return to familiar topics, you'll see them with fresh eyes and deeper understanding. Let this list support your ongoing growth and exploration.

- Being open
- Boundaries with spirit
- Building a Symbol dictionary
- Akashic records
- Creating connection with Spirit
- Is it my imagination?
- Opening/closing prayers
- Setting intentions
- Ways to protect yourself
- Why gratitude is important
- Why meditation is important
- Writing prayers
- Building your support network
- Direct/indirect messages
- Dive deeper into the senses
- Explore Natural Law
- Giving what you get
- Left/right brain
- Presentation Techniques
- Trusting what Spirit is giving you
- Understanding Relationships
- Unhooking information
- What to expect at a Psychic fair
- Why journaling is important
- Working with messages
- Candle/Smoke
- Channeling
- Flower or Ribbon Readings
- Past lives
- Physical mediumship
- Platform/Gallery
- Psychic Art
- Subjective vs. Objective
- Tea Leaves or Coffee Grounds
- Trance Mediumship
- Angels & Saints
- Animal Guides
- Meeting Spirit Guides
- Tying it all together
- What to charge for a reading
- Working through stage fright
- Astrology
- Chakras
- Diving Rods/Pendulums
- Numerology
- Runes
- Scrying
- Vision boards
- Working with Auras
- Tarot/Oracle Cards
- Forcing a connection with Spirit
- From the sitter's perspective
- Getting names/details
- Letting go of control
- Platform Techniques
- Supporting other practitioners

Books and Other Resources

In my first book, there is a selection of books that helped me on my journey to becoming a practicing Medium, That book *"Discovering Your Stream"* is widely available and a great resource for those just starting their journey. For every book listed there are at least 10 others out there. Don't be afraid to explore a variety of authors to help you along the way. Here are some books that helped me along the way and you may wish to read to help you:

Becoming a Spiritualist—H. Gordon Burroghs
Beginning Mediumship Workbook—Carole Anne
Companions in Spirit—Jack Grant
Divine Wisdom—Lisa Williams
Facilitating Learning with the Adult Brain in Mind—Kathleen Taylor
Five Paths of Student Engagement: - Dennis Shirley & Andy Hardgraves
Hot to Teach Adults—Dan Spalding
Life with Spirit—Sharon A. Klinger
Natural Brilliance: Overcoming any challenge .. At will—Paul R. Scheele
NSAC Spiritualist Manual
Pausing Long Enough to Notice—Theresa D. Huges
So You Want to Become a Medium—Rose Vanden Eynden
Spirit Circle Games: A guidebook for mediumship development circles—Rev. Joanna Bartlett
The Astrology of Time—Gary Goldschneider
The Psychic Workshop—Kim Chestney
The Question of God—Dr. Armand M. Nicholi, Jr.
The Ring of Chairs—Rev. Marilyn J. Awtry
The Spirit Animal Directory—Dawn Baumann Brunke
Transformational Breathwork: The Basics of Renewal and Rebirth—Patricia Price
When "Spiritual but Not Religious" is not Enough—Lillian Daniel

Spiritual Churches have lots of resources and often have libraries for their members. If you are ever fortunate to get to Lily Dale Assembly they have an amazing collection of books in their library. No matter if you are a participant or facilitator, your learning will never stop. Be curious, and explore the topics that you are drawn to. There is a reason, just trust you will find it when you need it.

The following people, in addition to Jack Rudy, over the years have had an influence on my ability to run effective circles, they include: Colin Bates, Dan Chesboro, Celeste Elliott, Carol Gasber, Tami Holbury-Ferraro, Cari Huston, Sharon Klinger, Terence Milne, John Paananen, Patricia Price, Judith Rochester, JoAnn Santonocito, Lady Shiya, Ronald Skowronski, John White, and Lisa Williams. Each has a very different style that I appreciate and love.

The good news — when you are ready the teacher will appear...

Notes

Introduction to Your 30-Day Spirit Awareness Journal

Welcome to your 30-Day Spirit Awareness Journal! This journal is designed to help you tune into your spiritual connections and become more aware of the subtle energies around you. By dedicating just a few minutes each day, you can deepen your spiritual practice and enhance your awareness of the unseen world.

How It Works

- **Daily Commitment**: Spend 5-10 minutes each day with your journal.
- **Write Three Observations**: Each day, write down three moments or experiences where you felt connected to spirit. These could be intuitive feelings, signs from loved ones, or moments of peace and clarity.
- **Include a Quick Reflection**: Next to each observation, jot down a brief reflection on what it meant to you or how it made you feel. This helps you build a deeper connection to your spiritual experiences.

Tips for Success

- **Stay Open**: Spirit can communicate in many ways—through thoughts, feelings, signs, or symbols. Stay open to the possibilities.
- **Consistency Matters**: Writing each day, even briefly, will help you strengthen your spiritual awareness and deepen your connection.
- **Reflect and Grow**: As you move through the 30 days, look back at your entries to see how your awareness and understanding have evolved.

By the end of this 30-day journey, you'll have a clearer sense of your spiritual connections and a deeper awareness of the spirit world around you. Let this journal be a tool to guide you on your spiritual path.

Happy journaling!

30 Day Spirit Awareness Journal

Date:

1.
2.
3.

Date:

1.
2.
3.

Date:

1.
2.
3.

Date:

1.
2.
3.

Date:

1.
2.
3.

Date:

1.
2.
3.

30 Day Spirit Awareness Journal

Date:

1.
2.
3.

Date:

1.
2.
3.

Date:

1.
2.
3.

Date:

1.
2.
3.

Date:

1.
2.
3.

Date:

1.
2.
3.

30 Day Spirit Awareness Journal

Date:

1.
2.
3.

Date:

1.
2.
3.

Date:

1.
2.
3.

Date:

1.
2.
3.

Date:

1.
2.
3.

Date:

1.
2.
3.

30 Day Spirit Awareness Journal

Date:

1.
2.
3.

Date:

1.
2.
3.

Date:

1.
2.
3.

Date:

1.
2.
3.

Date:

1.
2.
3.

Date:

1.
2.
3.

30 Day Spirit Awareness Journal

Date:

1.
2.
3.

Date:

1.
2.
3.

Date:

1.
2.
3.

Date:

1.
2.
3.

Date:

1.
2.
3.

Date:

1.
2.
3.

Gratitude Journal

Introduction to Your 30-Day Gratitude Journal

Welcome to your 30-Day Gratitude Journal! This journal is your space to build a simple but powerful habit of recognizing the good in your life. By spending just a few minutes each day, you can shift your mindset, increase your happiness, and bring more positivity into your world.

How It Works

- **Daily Commitment:** Set aside just 5-10 minutes each day.
- **Write Three Things:** Each day, write down three things you're grateful for. These can be big or small—anything that brings you joy, comfort, or a sense of peace.
- **Include a Quick Why:** Next to each item, jot down a quick reason why you're grateful for it. This helps deepen your appreciation and understanding.

Tips for Success

- **Keep It Simple:** Don't overthink it—gratitude can be found in the simplest moments.
- **Consistency is Key:** Try to write every day, even if it's just a few words. This habit is what creates lasting change.
- **Reflect Often:** As you progress, take a moment to look back on what you've written. You'll be amazed at how much there is to be grateful for.
-

By the end of these 30 days, you'll have a collection of gratitude that reflects the positive aspects of your life. Let this journal be a tool for bringing more joy and fulfillment into your daily routine.

Happy journaling!

30 Day Gratitude Journal

Date:

1.
2.
3.

Date:

1.
2.
3.

Date:

1.
2.
3.

Date:

1.
2.
3.

Date:

1.
2.
3.

Date:

1.
2.
3.

30 Day Gratitude Journal

Date:

1.
2.
3.

Date:

1.
2.
3.

Date:

1.
2.
3.

Date:

1.
2.
3.

Date:

1.
2.
3.

Date:

1.
2.
3.

30 Day Gratitude Journal

Date:

1.
2.
3.

Date:

1.
2.
3.

Date:

1.
2.
3.

Date:

1.
2.
3.

Date:

1.
2.
3.

Date:

1.
2.
3.

30 Day Gratitude Journal

Date:

1.
2.
3.

Date:

1.
2.
3.

Date:

1.
2.
3.

Date:

1.
2.
3.

Date:

1.
2.
3.

Date:

1.
2.
3.

30 Day Gratitude Journal

Date:

1.
2.
3.

Date:

1.
2.
3.

Date:

1.
2.
3.

Date:

1.
2.
3.

Date:

1.
2.
3.

Date:

1.
2.
3.

Notes